Collins

Mission: français

Workbook 2

Oliver Gray

Series Editor: Linzy Dickinson

William Collins's dream of knowledge for all began with the publication of his first book in 1819. A self-educated mill worker, he not only enriched millions of lives, but also founded a flourishing publishing house. Today, staying true to this spirit, Collins books are packed with inspiration, innovation and practical expertise. They place you at the centre of a world of possibility and give you exactly what you need to explore it.

Collins. Freedom to teach.

Published by Collins

An imprint of HarperCollins*Publishers*

77–85 Fulham Palace Road

Hammersmith

London

W6 8JB

Browse the complete Collins catalogue at
www.collins.co.uk

ISBN-13 978-0-00-751345-1

British Library Cataloguing in Publication Data

A Catalogue record for this publication is available from the British Library.

Commissioned by Katie Sergeant

Series concept by Linzy Dickinson

Project managed by Elektra Media Ltd

Development edited by Naomi Laredo

Copy-edited by Claire Trocmé

Concept design by Elektra Media Ltd

Illustrations by Elektra Media Ltd

Typeset by Jouve India Private Limited

Cover design by Angela English

Printed and bound by L.E.G.O. S.p.A. Italy

Acknowledgements

The publishers wish to thank the following for permission to reproduce photographs. Every effort has been made to trace copyright holders and to obtain their permission for the use of copyright materials. The publishers will gladly receive any information enabling them to rectify any error or omission at the first opportunity.

(t = top, c = centre, b = bottom, r = right, l = left)

Cover t Pecold/Shutterstock, cover cl Jacques PALUT/Shutterstock, cover cr Iuri/Shutterstock, cover b prochasson Frederic/Shutterstock, p 21tl senkaya/Shutterstock, p 21tcl Pressmaster/Shutterstock, p 21tcr dotshock/Shutterstock, p 21tr John Panella/Shutterstock, p 21bl Janine Wiedel Photolibrary/Alamy, p 21bcl Poznyakov/Shutterstock, p 21bcr AVAVA/Shutterstock, p 21r Joel Blit/Shutterstock, p 25tl margouillat photo/Shutterstock, p 25tc Lilyana Vynogradova/Shutterstock, p 25tr WM_idea/Shutterstock, p 25bl HLPhoto/Shutterstock, p 25bc Krzysztof Slusarczyk/Shutterstock, p 25br Lilyana Vynogradova/Shutterstock, p 31l julie deshaies/Shutterstock, p 31c Sukharevskyy Dmytro (nevodka)/Shutterstock, p 31r Irene Abdou/Alamy, p 34tl Jiri Hera/Shutterstock, p 34tcl Filipe B. Varela/Shutterstock, p 34tcr Ildi Papp/Shutterstock, p 34tr pick/Shutterstock, p 34bl bajinda/Shutterstock, p 34bcl Gyorgy Barna/Shutterstock, p 34bcr asharkyu/Shutterstock, p 34br Jag_cz/Shutterstock, p 36tl JOAT/Shutterstock, p 36tc Foodio/Shutterstock, p 36tr Foodpictures/Shutterstock, p 36bl Biosphoto/SuperStock, p 36br Foodpictures/Shutterstock, p 40tl ILYA AKINSHIN/Shutterstock, p 40tcl Roblan/Shutterstock, p 40tcr Jiri Hera/Shutterstock, p 40tr ffolas/Shutterstock, p 40bl Volosina/Shutterstock, p 40bcl Sea Wave/Shutterstock, p 40bcr stockcreations/Shutterstock, p 40br Melica/Shutterstock, p 41 fredredhat/Shutterstock, p 42l Harold Cunningham/Getty Images, p 42cl MARWAN NAAMANI/AFP/Getty Images, p 42c David Price/Arsenal FC via Getty Images, p 42cr Frederic Nebinger/WireImage/Getty Images, p 42r Vera Anderson/WireImage/Getty Images, p 45 BERTRAND LANGLOIS/AFP/Getty Images, p 47 Sarah M. Golonka/Getty Images, p 49 Christophe Testi/Shutterstock, p 50 syaochka/Shutterstock, p 51lt Vereshchagin Dmitry/Shutterstock, p 51ltc huyangshu/Shutterstock, p 51lbc B747/Shutterstock, p 51lb Mary Plage/Getty Images, p 51rt Daniel J. Rao/Shutterstock, p 51rc Prometheus72/Shutterstock, p 51rb De Agostini Picture Library/Getty Images, p 53 SEBASTIEN HREBLAY/AFP/Getty Images, p 59 Denizo71/Shutterstock, p 68 John Wollwerth/Shutterstock, p 70 AFP/Stringer/Getty Images, p 72tl Justin Setterfield/Getty Images, p 72tr Kevin C. Cox/Getty Images, p 72c Robert Hallam/BPI/Corbis, p 72bl BEN STANSALL/AFP/Getty Images, p 72br Dan Kitwood/Getty Images, p 73 Matt Turner/ALLSPORT/Getty Images, p 79 Musée Magritte Museum, p 83 amit mendelsohn/Demotix/Corbis, p 85 Face to Face/Photoshot, p 88 silky/Shutterstock, p 89t Featureflash/Shutterstock, p 89b cinemafestival/Shutterstock, p 95t Photobac/Shutterstock, p 95bl bikeriderlondon/Shutterstock, p 95bc oliveromg/Shutterstock, p 95br Kristy Sparow/Getty Images.

Mon autoportrait

Draw your self-portrait and complete the sentences below.

Je m'appelle _____ .

Ma classe est _____ .

Tableau des contenus

Exercise Key

reading　　writing　　listening　　speaking　　translation

• Pupil Book pages 8–9

Aujourd'hui, c'est le _____ . Il est _____ .

Langue et grammaire

The infinitive
The infinitive of a verb is the form it has when you look it up in a dictionary, before you change it. For example: *aller* (to go), *avoir* (to have) and *apprendre* (to learn). Here are some of the ways it is used.

Saying what you want to do
Remember that to say what you want or don't want to do you can use the verb *vouloir* followed by another verb in the infinitive form:

Je veux aller au parc. — I want to go to the park.
Je ne veux pas faire mes devoirs. — I don't want to do my homework.

The near future
Remember: to talk about what you are going to do in the near future you can use the verb *aller* followed by an infinitive:

Demain je vais retrouver mes copains. — Tomorrow I'm going to see my friends again.
Samedi nous allons visiter le musée. — On Saturday, we're going to visit the museum.

Giving instructions
You can use the infinitive when writing instructions. For example:

Ne pas manger. — Do not eat.

 1 What's good and bad about going back to school? Put a tick by the good things and a cross by the bad things.

a Je veux rester à la maison. _____X_____

b Je ne veux pas travailler. _____

c On va retrouver les copains. _____

d On va se lever de bonne heure. _____

e Nous allons faire beaucoup de devoirs. _____

f Je veux jouer pendant la récré. _____

g On va beaucoup apprendre. _____

h Je veux aller au collège. _____

 2 Re-read exercise 1. Which sentences say what will happen and which say what the person wants to happen? Write '**will**' or '**want**'.

a want _____ b _____

c _____ d _____

e _____ f _____

g _____ h _____

Identify the infinitive in each sentence in exercise 1. Write down the infinitives and their English translations.

a _rester, to stay_____   b _____

c _____   d _____

e _____   f _____

g _____   h _____

 Unjumble these pieces of advice and write them under the appropriate picture.

1

_____

_____

2

_____

_____

3

_____

_____

4

_____

_____

5

_____

_____

6

_____

_____

a un déjeuner. Prendre petit bon   **b** les soir. Préparer le vêtements

c avec copains. Jouer les   **d** 7h. lever Se à

e copains. les avec Aller collège au   **f** scolaire. le Préparer materiel

 A chooses a piece of advice from exercise 4 and reads it out. B agrees to do it. Then swap roles.

Exemple

A Jouer avec les copains.

B Oui, je vais jouer avec les copains.

6 Read the sentences and write *Canada, France* or *Nouvelle-Calédonie.*

a La rentrée, c'est au mois de septembre.   _____

b Les grandes vacances sont en décembre.   _____

c La rentrée, c'est au mois d'août.   _____

d La rentrée, c'est au mois de février.   _____

e L'été est en janvier!   _____

7 Read the text and answer the questions in a few words. ⭐

> Je m'appelle Antoine et j'habite en Nouvelle-Calédonie. Ici, la rentrée est au mois de février. Les grandes vacances sont en décembre et janvier, parce que c'est l'été. Maintenant, c'est la fin des vacances et je veux aller au collège parce que je vais retrouver mes copains et je veux jouer pendant la récré. Je ne veux pas faire les devoirs, bien sûr, mais ce n'est pas grave!

a Où habite Antoine?   _____

b C'est quand, la rentrée?   _____

c C'est quand, les grandes vacances?   _____

d Qu'est-ce qu'il veut faire pendant la récré? _____

e Qu'est-ce qu'il ne veut pas faire?   _____

 8 Translate into French, using an infinitive in each sentence. ⭐

a I will meet my friends.   _____

b I want to learn a lot.   _____

c I don't want to do my homework.   _____

d We will work a lot.   _____

e I want to play during break.   _____

f We will have a good breakfast.   _____

• Pupil Book pages 10–11

Aujourd'hui, c'est le _____ . Il est _____ .

Langue et grammaire

Describing a sequence of events

Some adverbs help to describe the order you did things in. They're easy to use and will make your French seem more fluent. Three very useful adverbs are:

d'abord	first
ensuite	then
après	after

The perfect tense – a reminder

Use the perfect tense to talk about something you did in the past. To form the perfect tense, for most verbs you use the present tense of the verb *avoir* and the past participle.

For a small number of verbs, you use *être* instead:

J'ai joué avec mes copains.   I played with my friends.
Nous avons joué au foot.   We played football.

Je suis allé(e) en Italie.   I went to Italy.
Elle est allée en Espagne.   She went to Spain.

Using *c'est* and *c'était*

You can use *c'est* with an adjective to describe an experience:

Je n'aime pas aller au bord de la mer – c'est nul!
I don't like going to the seaside – it's rubbish!

With a determiner (*le, la, un, une, mon, ma*, etc.), you can use it to point out a specific person or thing:

C'est une péniche.   It's a barge
C'est mon oncle.   That's my uncle.

To say what an experience was like, use *c'était*:

Hier j'ai joué au foot – c'était génial!
Yesterday I played football – it was great!

 1 Decide whether each of these places is a country (*pays*) or a region of France (*région*). Write *P* or *R*.

a États-Unis ▢   b Pays Basque ▢

c Dordogne ▢   d Italie ▢

e Maroc ▢   f Espagne ▢

g Bretagne ▢   h Provence ▢

i Angleterre ▢

 2 Would you put *en*, *au* or *aux* in front of the countries and regions in exercise 1?

a _____   b _____

c _____   d _____

e _____   f _____

g _____   h _____

i _____

3 Test your French geography. Copy the names of the regions onto the labels.

Provence　　Pays Basque　　Normandie　　Bretagne　　Dordogne

a _____

b _____

c _____

d _____

e _____

4 Solve the clues and write in the words. What is the mystery word?

a Region on the French–Spanish border

b Region in the south of France

c European country shaped like a boot

d North American country

e Country near Spain

f Country near Portugal

g Holiday region in central France

h Hot country with capital Athens

Mystery word = _____

5 Fill in each gap with the correct past participle from the box.

joué　　mangé　　allée　　passé　　allées　　visité

J'ai_____un week-end génial en Belgique.

Je suis_____à Bruxelles. D'abord nous

avons_____un musée et ensuite nous

avons_____des moules dans un restaurant.

Après, nous sommes_____au parc et nous

avons_____au foot.

6 In pairs, take it in turns to ask and answer these questions.

- Tu as passé les vacances en France ou à l'étranger?

- Tu es allé(e) où?

- Qu'est-ce que tu as fait?

7 Read this text and answer the questions in English. ⭐

J'ai passé les vacances avec ma famille en Espagne. Nous sommes allés à Bilbao, dans le nord de l'Espagne. En général, c'était génial. D'abord, nous avons visité le musée Guggenheim. Pour moi, c'était un peu ennuyeux parce que je n'aime pas l'art moderne. Ensuite, nous avons mangé dans un restaurant dans le centre-ville. La paella était délicieuse. Après, nous avons fait de la planche à voile. J'ai trouvé ça très amusant mais fatigant aussi. L'hôtel était confortable mais un peu cher.

a Where is Bilbao? _____

b Did Félix go there alone? _____

c What's his opinion of modern art? _____

d Where was the restaurant? _____

e What did he eat? _____

f What did they do in the afternoon? _____

g How did he feel about it? _____

h What did he think of the hotel? _____

8 Write a short account of a holiday like Félix's in exercise 7. Include: ⭐

- where you went

- who you went with

- what you did (at least three things)

- what you thought of it.

Remember to make the past participle agree if you are using '*être* verbs'. For example:

- nous sommes allées (two or more females)

- nous sommes allés (mixed group of people).

- Pupil Book pages 12–13

Aujourd'hui, c'est le _____ . Il est _____ .

Langue et grammaire

Expressing opinions

There are many ways of expressing your opinion. Do you remember these?

Je pense que...	I think that…
Je trouve que...	I find that…
À mon avis...	In my opinion…

When you're saying what you think about something it's useful to be able to explain why. You can do this by using intensifiers like *très, un peu,* or *trop.*

Elle est un peu timide. She is a little shy.

Quelquefois il est   Sometimes he is
   trop impatient.   too impatient.

You can also use *plus ... que* and *moins ... que* to compare things. Look at these examples:

Sophie est plus raisonnable   Sophie is more
   que Lucas.   sensible than Lucas.

Abdou est moins bavard   Abdou is less chatty
   que Justine   than Justine.

Pronunciation

Remember that if you see é in a word, it must be pronounced even if it comes before another vowel. For example, the *éa* in *idéaliste* is heard as two separate vowels.

1 In the grid, find ten adjectives which express opinions. The words are given in English in the green box.

r	é	a	l	i	s	t	e	a	h	i
a	b	n	t	o	é	f	i	a	i	d
i	h	g	n	k	r	r	f	i	d	é
s	x	r	m	f	i	a	b	l	e	a
o	p	a	r	j	e	p	s	s	a	l
n	e	i	o	j	u	s	t	e	e	i
n	j	s	é	z	x	r	t	p	s	s
a	u	l	p	a	m	u	s	a	n	t
b	ê	t	e	i	v	a	u	c	r	e
l	c	b	a	m	u	s	p	l	f	m
e	p	a	r	e	s	s	e	u	x	l
d	e	i	d	é	a	p	r	h	a	d

serious

fun

reliable

fair

stupid

sensible

realistic

idealistic

lazy

super

2 Write the French words in the gaps.

_____ _____ _____ (*In my opinion*), Abdou est _____ _____ (*more reliable*) que Félix.

_____ _____ _____ (*I think that*) Luc est _____ _____ (*less serious*) que Maeva.

_____ _____ _____ (*I find that*) Thomas est _____ _____ (*less realistic*) que Lucas.

3 Which sentences say the person **wants** to do something and which say the person **will** do something? Write 'want' or 'will'.

a Je veux aller en Angleterre. _____

b Je vais faire mes devoirs. _____

c Je veux être délégué de classe. _____

d Je veux utiliser mon portable. _____

e Je vais voter pour Thomas. _____

f Je vais voter pour Manon. _____

4 Write in the missing words.

a Manon est _____ _____ que Sophie. *(more reliable)*

b Sophie est _____ _____ que Manon. *(less sensible)*

c Lucas est _____ _____ qu'Abdou. *(more realistic)*

d Abdou est _____ _____ que Thomas. *(less fair)*

e Thomas est _____ _____ que Lucas. *(more serious)*

5 Translate Lucas's manifesto into English. ⭐

_____

_____

_____

_____

_____

_____

_____

_____

_____

ÉLECTION

délégué de classe

Vote pour moi si tu veux:
* ★ utiliser les ordinateurs plus souvent
* ★ faire plus de sport l'après-midi
* ★ avoir trois mois de vacances
* ★ abolir les devoirs
* ★ aller en Amérique en voyage de classe
* ★ manger des frites pendant la récré

Lucas

6 Which of his promises are realistic? Discuss them with your classmates in English and make some notes.

_____

_____

_____

_____

7 Speak in pairs. A asks the questions below. B answers using the words in the box and any 'opinion' adjectives he or she can think of. Then swap roles.

• Que penses-tu de Lucas?

• Et qu'est-ce que tu penses de ses idées?

• Pourquoi?

| Je pense que... | Je trouve que... | À mon avis... | très / un peu / trop |

8 Now write your own manifesto for an election as class representative. Use any vocabulary from this Workbook or your Pupil Book. If you need more, use a dictionary or ask your teacher. ⭐

_____

_____

_____

_____

_____

_____

_____

• Pupil Book pages 14–15

Aujourd'hui, c'est le _____ . Il est _____ .

Langue et grammaire

Saying what you can do

The verb *pouvoir* means 'to be able'. To talk about what you can do, use the *on* form of this verb:

On peut parler avec des copains.	You can talk to friends.
On peut jouer en ligne.	You can play online.

The imperative

You use the imperative form of a verb to tell someone what to do. If you are speaking to more than one person, use the *vous* form of the verb, but without the word *vous*:

Écoutez tout le monde.	Listen everyone.
Pensez à notre planète.	Think of our planet.
Ne parlez pas.	Don't speak.

Note that some verbs, like the verb *être*, have irregular imperative forms:

Soyez gentils!	Be kind!
Ne soyez pas impatients.	Don't be impatient.

Giving advice

The phrase *Il est important de…* means 'It is important to…'. You can follow this phrase with any verb in its infinitive form:

Il est important de considérer l'effet.	It is important to consider the effect.

Pronunciation

Notice how the letters *–ion* at the end of a word are pronounced slightly differently in French. For example, compare the English word 'connection' with the French *connexion*.

 Fill in the English words in this dictionary extract.

_____ Dictionnaire de _____ la technologie

chatter *v* to __chat__

connexion *f* a _____

contacter *v* to _____

émission *f* a _____

envoyer *v* to _____

partager *v* to _____

poster *v* to _____

texto *m* a _____

2

2 Unjumble these sentences. They all begin with *On peut...*

a peut blogs. des On lire _____

b envoyer On texto. peut un _____

c contacter peut copains. On les _____

d l'Internet. peut On à accès avoir _____

e cybercafé. peut au On aller _____

f en On sociaux. rester peut les sur contact réseaux _____

g trouver On informations. peut des _____

h photos. peut On des partager _____

3 Now translate the sentences in exercise 2 into English.

a _____

b _____

c _____

d _____

e _____

f _____

g _____

h _____

4 With a partner, work out how you would give these instructions to a group of people. Say the instructions out loud.

a Pay attention.

b Speak to an adult.

c Be nice.

d Think about the images.

e Don't stay online.

5 True or false? Write 'T' or 'F'.

> Moi, j'adore les réseaux sociaux. On peut chatter avec des copains et on peut partager des photos aussi. C'est génial, ça! On peut exprimer des opinions sur l'école, sur le sport, sur la politique. On peut rester en contact avec des amis, même si on n'est pas à la maison, parce qu'on peut se connecter avec un portable. Moi, quand je rentre à la maison en autobus, je chatte avec ma copine qui est au collège!

a Gabriel likes social networks. _____   **b** He never shares photos. _____

c He likes discussing politics. _____   **d** He doesn't talk about school. _____

e He has a girlfriend. _____   **f** He's interested in sport. _____

g He only uses social networks at home. _____

6 Write down, in English, at least four things Gabriel says you **can** do.

_____

_____

_____

_____

7 Read the text and answer the questions.

> Le week-end dernier a été une catastrophe. Je suis allée à une fête où j'ai dansé comme une idiote. Ma «copine» a fait des photos de moi avec son portable. Elle a posté les photos sur Internet. Oh, là, là! Tout le monde a vu les photos, même mes parents! Le week-end prochain je vais rester à la maison. Je ne vais pas regarder les réseaux sociaux.

a When did this happen? _____

b What did Amandine do? _____

c What did her friend do? _____

d Who saw the result? _____

e What does she resolve to do? _____

8 Make a list in French of things you can do using new technology. Use *On peut…* Use any vocabulary from this Workbook or your Pupil Book. Also give a couple of tips for online behaviour, using the imperative form: *pensez, restez, soyez,* etc.

• Pupil Book pages 16–17

Aujourd'hui, c'est le _____ . Il est _____ .

Langue et grammaire

Suggesting where to go

To suggest going somewhere, you can use the expression *Si on allait…?* This is like saying 'What about going to…? Look at these examples:
Si on allait à la plage?   What about going to the beach?
Si on allait au cinéma?   What about going to the cinema?

Saying no to a suggestion

To say 'no' to a suggestion because you have to do something else, use the verb *devoir* (to have to) followed by the infinitive of another verb:
Je dois rendre visite à   I have to visit my cousins.
   mes cousins.

To reject a suggestion because you'd prefer something else, use the verb *préférer* followed by a noun or the infinitive of another verb:
Je préfère la musique classique.
Je préfère aller au cinéma.

Arranging where to meet

Use the following phrases to describe where to meet people. Remember to change *de* depending on whether the place you are talking about is masculine or feminine:
à côté de la piscine   next to the swimming pool
près du cinéma   near the cinema

---

 1   Write in *au* or *à la*.

a _____ piscine   b _____ parc   c _____ café

d _____ bibliothèque   e _____ cinéma   f _____ centre-ville

g _____ restaurant   h _____ patinoire   i _____ skate-parc

j _____ plage   k _____ tour Eiffel   l _____ collège

masculine: café   centre-ville   cinéma   collège   parc   restaurant   skate-parc
feminine: bibliothèque   patinoire   piscine   plage   tour Eiffel

2   Unjumble these sentences to make suggestions.

Thomas

Sophie

Maeva

a   au allait Si parc? on   _____

b   on plage? à allait Si la   _____

c   on Si ville? centre au allait _____

d   à allait Si la on patinoire? _____

e   allait Si bibliothèque? à on la _____

3 In pairs. A writes down a place they'd like to go to using words from this topic. B makes suggestions using *Si on allait…?* When he or she mentions the place A has chosen, A says *D'accord!* Then swap roles.

4 Draw a simple labelled map of the area described in the text. When you have finished, compare your map with the ones some of your classmates have drawn. How similar or different are they?

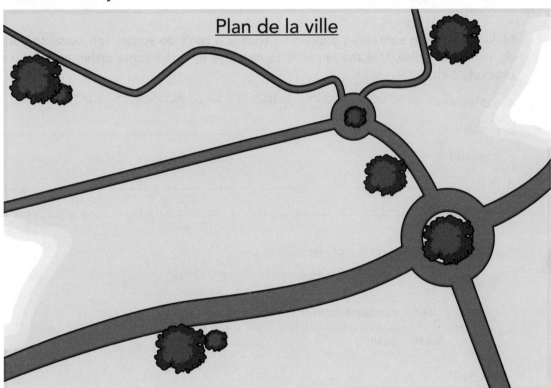

Plan de la ville

La piscine est près du parc et le café est à côté de la piscine. Le restaurant est en face du skate-parc. Le cinéma est à côté du collège et le collège est près de la piscine.

5 Translate these phrases into French, using *du* or *de la*.

a near the swimming pool _____

b next to the park _____

c opposite the cinema _____

d near the town centre _____

e next to the beach _____

f opposite the ice rink _____

masculine: centre-ville   cinéma   parc
feminine: patinoire   piscine   plage

6 Draw lines to match up the French sentences with the descriptions in English.

1 Someone who has schoolwork to do.

2 Someone who has to visit a relative.

3 Someone who has to do some shopping.

4 Someone who has to listen to some music.

5 Someone with toothache.

a Je dois rendre visite à ma tante.

b Je dois aller au concert.

c Je dois aller chez le dentiste.

d Je dois faire mes devoirs.

e Je dois aller au supermarché.

 7 Make some long sentences explaining that you can't do something because you have to do something else. Use the answers to exercise 6, in the same order, and the words in brackets below. ⭐

a *(patinoire)* _Je ne peux pas aller à la patinoire parce que je dois faire mes devoirs._

b *(café)* _____

c *(piscine)* _____

d *(parc)* _____

e *(cinéma)* _____

8 True or false? Write 'T' or 'F'. ⭐

Sur:	marc@marcmail.fr
Sujet:	Salut!

Salut Marc!

Malheureusement, je ne peux pas aller au cinéma ce soir parce que je dois rendre visite à mon oncle. Moi, je préfère un rendez-vous demain matin en face du centre sportif. On pourrait aller au café. Ça te va?

Olivier

a Olivier would like to meet Marc in town. _____

b He will visit Marc's uncle. _____

c He'd like to meet up tomorrow morning. _____

d He says the sports centre is near the cinema. _____

e He wants to meet up for coffee this evening. _____

The answers aren't always the obvious ones, so think carefully.

• Pupil Book pages 18–19

Aujourd'hui, c'est le _____ . Il est _____ .

Langue et grammaire

Ordinal numbers

Ordinal numbers are used to talk about order and position, for example 'first' and 'second'. In French, there is both a masculine and a feminine form of the word for 'first'. The other ordinal numbers don't change. Use *au* to say 'on' a floor.

au premier étage	on the first floor
la première fois	the first time
au deuxième étage	on the second floor
la deuxième fois	the second time
au troisième étage	on the third floor
la troisième fois	the third time

Using the imperative

As you know, the imperative is used to tell someone what to do. When you are speaking directly to a person you know well, use the *tu* form of the present tense of a verb, without the *tu*. For –*er* verbs you also take the letter *s* off the end. For example: *Monte au premier étage.* Go up to the first floor.

Using *il* and *elle*

Il and *elle* are *pronouns*. They stand in place of a noun. Use *il* and *elle* (and not *c'est*) when the person reading or listening already knows which particular noun (person or thing) they are being used in place of: *il* for a masculine noun, and *elle* for a feminine noun.

Tu cherches le théâtre? Il est à côté du cinéma.
Are you looking for the theatre? It's next to the cinema.
Où est la salle d'histoire? Elle est au premier étage.
Where is the history classroom? It's on the second floor.

1 Draw lines to link the pictures to the words that describe them.

  (photo)

le CDI   la cour

la salle des profs   le gymnase

la cantine   les toilettes

les laboratoires   la salle de classe

2 The numbers in the pictures in exercise 1 tell you which floor they are on. Complete the sentences.

a Les laboratoires sont au troisième étage.

b Le gymnase est _____ _____ _____.

c Les toilettes sont _____ _____ _____.

d Le CDI est _____ _____ _____.

e La salle des profs est _____ _____ _____.

f La cantine est _____ _____ _____.

 3 Work out which room is which and write the names of the rooms on the plan.

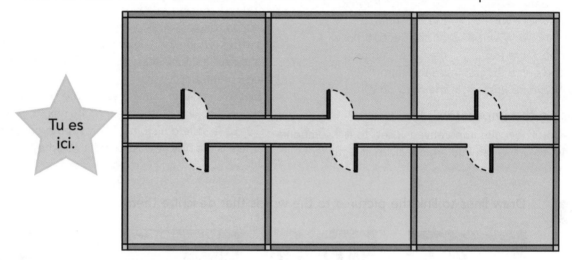

Tu es ici.

a La salle d'histoire? – La deuxième porte à gauche.

b La cantine? – La première porte à droite.

c Le gymnase? – La troisième porte à gauche.

d La bibliothèque? – La première porte à gauche.

e La salle d'anglais? – La troisième porte à droite.

f La salle de musique? – La deuxième porte à droite.

 4 Draw a plan like the one in exercise 3, but put the rooms in different places. Draw a second plan, leaving the rooms blank. A asks where the places are by saying *C'est où, la cantine*? B replies *C'est la ... porte à ...* A writes the name of the room on the blank plan. At the end, check that your plans are identical. Then swap roles.

5 Circle the correct imperative form.

a Prend / Prends le couloir.

b Monte / Montes au premier étage.

c Descend / Descends au rez-de-chaussée.

d Continues / Continue tout droit.

e Tourne / Tournes à droite.

6 What directions does Maeva give to Kimi? Write them down in English. ⭐

Alors, Kimi, ne t'inquiète pas! Pour trouver la salle d'informatique, prends le couloir et c'est la première porte à gauche. Pour trouver la salle des profs, monte au premier étage, prends le couloir et c'est la première porte à droite. Et pour trouver la cantine, descends au rez-de-chaussée. Prends le couloir et c'est la troisième porte à gauche. Tu vois, c'est facile!

_____

_____

_____

_____

7 Translate into French. ⭐

a Go up to the first floor. Take the corridor and it's the second door on the left.

_____

b Go down to the ground floor. Take the corridor and it's the third door on the right.

_____

• Pupil Book pages 32–33

Aujourd'hui, c'est le _____ . Il est _____ .

Langue et grammaire

The definite article

When talking about food that you like and dislike, remember to use the definite article, which can be *le*, *la*, *l'* or *les*:

J'adore le poisson.	I love fish.
Je déteste la viande.	I hate meat.
Je déteste l'ail.	I hate garlic.
Je craque pour les fruits de mer.	I can't resist seafood.
Mon péché mignon, c'est le chocolat.	I have a weakness for chocolate.

Talking about ingredients

To talk about the ingredients in a dish, it is important to remember that words expressing a quantity are followed by *de*. Not *du*, not *de la*, not *des*; just *de*!

*un plat **de** poisson*	a fish dish
*beaucoup **de** légumes*	lots of vegetables

Pronunciation

Notice how the letters *ouill* are pronounced, for example in *bouillabaisse*.

---

1 Solve the clues. Copy out the words from the box below.

fruits de mer	dessert	poisson	frites	haricots	légumes	viande	soupe

a Something you eat after the main course   _____

b Eat five portions a day of these!   _____

c Not suitable for vegetarians   _____

d Liquid food!   _____

e Cockles and mussels   _____

f Fishy business!   _____

g Nice with a burger   _____

h Full of beans   _____

2 Write in *le*, *la*, *les* or *l'*. Genders are given below.

a _____ haricots   **b** _____ viande   **c** _____ poisson   **d** _____ dessert

e _____ moules   **f** _____ légumes   **g** _____ soupe   **h** _____ plat

> **masculine:** poisson plat dessert
> **feminine:** soupe viande
> **plural:** moules haricots légumes

3 Work out which dish is which. Write the name of the dish by each picture.

a

_____

b

_____

c

_____

d

_____

e

_____

f

_____

> **moules-frites** = fruits de mer
> **plateau de fromages** = camembert, gruyère, etc.
> **raclette** = fromage fondu
> **bouillabaisse** = une soupe de poissons
> **cassoulet** = un plat de haricots avec de la viande
> **clafoutis** = un dessert aux cerises

4 In pairs. A says the name of a dish or an item from exercise 3. B says what it is in English and also judges whether A has said it correctly. Then swap roles.

Be careful, as some of the words are hard to pronounce, e.g. bouillabaisse.
If the last letter of a French word is a consonant, it isn't usually pronounced, as in cassoulet, clafoutis.

5 Write sentences saying what Théo thinks about food.

> J'aime = √
> J'adore = √√
> Je craque pour = √√√
> Je n'aime pas = X
> Je déteste = XX

J'aime le _____

_____

_____

_____

_____

6   Answer the questions in English.

> Moi, j'adore les desserts. Mon dessert préféré, c'est le clafoutis aux cerises, mais j'adore aussi les gâteaux et les glaces. Je suis végétarienne, donc je ne mange pas de viande. Je déteste les burgers. Je craque pour le fromage et j'aime aussi les salades et le cassoulet – sans viande, c'est évident!

a Is Sophie a vegetarian?   _____

b What's her main food weakness?   _____

c Is she a fan of cakes?   _____

d What does she particularly hate?   _____

e What other desserts does she like?   _____

f How can she eat cassoulet?   _____

7   Translate the second half of Sophie's speech bubble into English, starting from *Je suis végétarienne...* ⭐

_____

_____

_____

_____

8   Write a few lines in French about what you like and don't like eating using the expressions from exercise 5. If you need extra vocabulary, ask your teacher or use a dictionary. ⭐

_____

_____

_____

_____

• Pupil Book pages 34–35

Aujourd'hui, c'est le _____ . Il est _____ .

Langue et grammaire

Saying 'some'

The words 'some' and 'any' are often left out in English. However, you can't leave them out in French. Use:

du with masculine nouns
de la with feminine nouns
de l' before a vowel
des with plural nouns

Je voudrais du pain et de l'eau. I'd like some bread and water.

After a negative, *un, une, du, de la, de l'* and *des* all change to *de*:
Je n'ai pas de fourchette. I don't have a fork.

Using *on*

You already know that the word *on* is often used to mean 'we'. It can also be used to mean 'people':

En France, on mange beaucoup de pain. In France, people eat a lot of bread.

Adverbs

Many French adverbs end in *–ment*; it's the equivalent of *–ly* in English.

directement	directly
généralement	generally
normalement	normally
seulement	only

Pouvoir + infinitive

Remember, you can follow the present tense of the verb *pouvoir* (to be able to) with a verb in its infinitive form to make requests or to ask for permission:

Je peux avoir du sucre? Can I have some sugar?

Tu peux me passer de l'eau? Can you pass me some water?

 Unjumble these words connected with food and write them under the correct pictures.

lob	tercetofuh	truayo	seaeitst	outueca	féca	ldasea	les	cruse	niap

a

_____

b

_____

c

_____

d

_____

e

_____

f

_____

g

_____

h

_____

i

_____

j

_____

2 Write in *du, de la, de l'* or *des.*

a Je voudrais _____ eau.

b Je voudrais _____ légumes.

c Je voudrais _____ fraises.

d Je voudrais _____ sucre.

e Je voudrais _____ viande.

f Je voudrais _____ pain.

g Je voudrais _____ poisson.

h Je voudrais _____ salade.

masculine: sucre   pain   poisson
feminine: viande   salade   eau
plural: légumes   fraises

3 In pairs. You've chosen a rubbish shop: it has run out of everything! A makes a request from exercise 2 and B replies. Then swap roles.

Exemple

A Je voudrais…

B Je regrette, je n'ai pas de…

4 Draw lines to link the French and English adverbs.

lentement	only
directement	generally
généralement	unfortunately
normalement	slowly
malheureusement	directly
seulement	normally

5 Find the French expressions in the text and write them down.

Souvent, le week-end, on fait un pique-nique dans le parc. On prend un panier avec du pain, du fromage et des tomates. On fait des sandwichs mais on ne les met pas sur une assiette. On les mange à la main! Après, on boit du jus d'orange et on mange un yaourt ou un fruit. J'adore les pique-niques, surtout quand il fait beau!

a some bread _____

b some cheese _____

c some tomatoes _____

d some sandwiches _____

e some orange juice _____

6 Translate the last two sentences (starting with *Après...*) into English. Remember that *on* can mean 'we' or 'people'. ⭐

_____

_____

7 Invent dialogues with a partner. A asks B to pass something and B responds. Remember that you will both need to use *du, de la, de l'* or *des*. Then swap roles. ⭐

Exemple

A Tu peux me passer..., s'il te plaît? **B** Voilà...

8 What do you remember about French meals?

a What is strange about the way breakfast is eaten?

_____

b What is unusual about how bread is served?

_____

c What is a common starter at lunchtime?

_____

d What is normally the last thing eaten at lunch or dinner?

_____

• Pupil Book pages 36–37

Aujourd'hui, c'est le _____ . Il est _____ .

Langue et grammaire

Adjectival agreement

Remember, French adjectives agree with the noun they describe.

• For most adjectives, just add an *e* to describe a feminine noun.
• If the adjective already ends in *–e*, there's no need to add another.
• Adjectives ending in *–ien* change to *–ienne*.
• Adjectives ending in *–if* change to *–ive*.

	Masculine singular	feminine singular
Sudanese	*soudanais*	*soudanaise*
Muslim	*musulman*	*musulmane*
allergic	*allergique*	*allergique*
Vietnamese	*vietnamien*	*vietnamienne*
vegetarian	*végétarien*	*végétarienne*
Jewish	*juif*	*juive*

When adjectives are introduced with *c'est* and not followed by a noun, they remain masculine singular.
C'est bon.   It's good.
C'est énervant.   It's annoying.

Talking about what you are allergic to

When using the phrase *allergique à*, remember to change *à* depending on the noun that follows.
allergique au fromage   allergic to cheese
allergique à la pénicilline   allergic to penicillin
allergique aux noisettes   allergic to hazelnuts

To say you never do something, use *ne … jamais*.
Elle ne boit jamais   She never
  de café.   drinks coffee.

---

1 Write in *au*, *à la*, *à l'* or *aux*.

a Je suis allergique _____ noisettes.

b Tu es allergique _____ lait?

c Victor est allergique _____ noix.

d Élise est allergique _____ fromage.

e Léon est allergique _____ pénicilline.

f Colette est allergique _____ curry.

g Akim est allergique _____ viande.

> **masculine:** lait   fromage   curry
> **feminine:** pénicilline   viande
> **plural:**   noix   noisettes

2 Circle the correct form of the adjective.

a J'adore la cuisine vietnamien / vietnamienne.

b Abdou est musulman / musulmane.

c Je préfère la cuisine français / française.

d Marc est végétarien / végétarienne.

e Rachelle est juif / juive.

f L'aloco poulet, c'est un plat soudanais / soudanaise.

3 Draw lines to link the sentence halves.

a Je ne mange pas de pain

b Je ne mange pas de porc

c Lola ne mange pas de moules

d Samir ne mange pas de porc

e Je ne mange pas de poulet

f Marine ne boit pas de chocolat chaud

parce que je suis végétarien.

parce qu'elle est allergique aux produits laitiers.

parce que je suis juive.

parce qu'elle est allergique aux fruits de mer.

parce qu'il est musulman.

parce que je ne dois pas manger de gluten.

4 Choose the correct French expression for each of these dishes from the box below.

a Vietnamese chicken sandwich _____

b Sudanese chicken dish _____

c dairy products _____

d Vietnamese pork sandwich _____

e Sudanese fish dish _____

l'aloco poulet   un banh mi au porc   un banh mi au poulet   l'aloco poisson   produits laitiers

5 Identify the French expressions in exercise 4 that correspond to these pictures. Copy them underneath the correct picture.

a

_____

_____

b

_____

_____

c

_____

_____

6   In pairs. A offers food to B. B replies that he/she never eats that food. Then swap roles.

Exemple

A Tu veux de la viande?

B Je ne mange jamais de viande.

7   Write five sentences about food you never eat: *Je ne mange jamais de...* ⭐
If you like everything, make it up!

_____

_____

_____

_____

_____

8   Read about Mehdi's family and fill in the gaps in the sentences. ⭐

Les repas chez nous sont problématiques. On est musulmans, alors on ne mange pas de porc. Ma soeur est végétarienne, donc elle ne mange pas de viande. Maman a la maladie coeliaque et elle ne mange jamais de pain. Papa est allergique aux noisettes et moi, je n'aime pas les fruits et les légumes. Mais tout le monde aime les oeufs!

a Mehdi's sister doesn't eat _____ because _____.

b Mehdi's mother doesn't eat _____ because _____.

c Mehdi's father doesn't eat _____ because _____.

d Mehdi doesn't eat _____ because _____.

e None of them eat _____ because _____.

f All of them eat _____ because _____.

• Pupil Book pages 38–39

Aujourd'hui, c'est le _____ . Il est _____ .

Langue et grammaire

Describing flavours

Some of the intensifiers you know already can be used to express quantities:

C'est assez sucré.	It's quite sweet.
C'est un peu épicé.	It's a bit spicy.
C'est trop amer.	It's too bitter.

Il n'y a pas assez de sucre.	There isn't enough sugar.
Tu as un peu de citron?	Have you got a bit of lemon?
Il y a trop de sel.	There's too much salt.

Use au, à la, à l' or aux to introduce the name of the filling or flavour:

une tarte **au** citron (m)	a lemon tart
un gâteau **à la** carotte (f)	a carrot cake
une glace **à l'**ananas (vowel)	a pineapple ice cream
une pizza **aux** champignons (p)	a mushroom pizza.

Saying what you'd like

When asking a friend whether they want something, use the present tense of vouloir:

Tu veux un peu de sucre?	Do you want a little sugar?

When answering, it is more polite to use je voudrais than je veux:

Je voudrais un peu de sel.	I would like a little salt.

Pronunciation

Remember that th in French is always pronounced like a 't'. For example le thé and le thon.

 Find and circle the eight food words in this wordsearch.

g	l	a	c	e	f	v
i	z	c	i	r	b	a
n	a	r	t	h	o	n
g	f	e	r	a	t	i
e	j	v	o	n	r	l
m	i	e	n	a	s	l
b	s	t	é	n	v	e
r	o	t	c	a	f	é
e	d	e	h	s	l	x

Write the words you have found in exercise 1 under the correct pictures.

a

b

c

d

_____

_____

_____

_____

e

f

g

h

_____

_____

_____

_____

Write in *au*, *à la*, *à l'* or *aux*.

a Une glace _____ vanille.

b Une glace _____ noisettes.

c Une glace _____ gingembre.

d Une glace _____ ananas.

e Une glace _____ chocolat.

f Une pizza _____ jambon.

g Une pizza _____ mozzarella.

h Une pizza _____ thon.

i Une pizza _____ crevettes.

j Une pizza _____ champignons.

> **masculine:** chocolat   gingembre   jambon   thon
> **feminine:**   vanille   mozzarella
> The rest you can work out, because they are plural or start with a vowel.

In pairs. Take it in turns to make up some horrible pizzas and ice creams. See if you can agree which is the most disgusting.

Exemple

A Je voudrais une glace / pizza au / à la / à l' / aux…

B C'est dégueulasse, ça!

Write in *C'est sucré/acide/épicé/amer/salé.*

a un gâteau au chocolat   _____

b des crevettes au curry   _____

c un citron   _____

d un café noir _____

e des frites _____

f une glace à la fraise _____

g du chili con carne _____

h des chips _____

 Translate into English.

a pas assez de sucre _____

b trop de sel _____

c un peu épicé _____

d un peu amer _____

e trop de piment rouge _____

7 **Translate into French.** ⭐

a an apple tart _____

b a cheese omelette _____

c a chocolate cake _____

d a strawberry mousse _____

8 **Read the text and circle 'T' (true) or 'F' (false).** ⭐

Hier soir, on est allés manger dans un restaurant indien. Moi, j'adore la cuisine indienne, mais mon poulet au curry était vraiment trop épicé! J'ai bu trois bouteilles d'eau et j'ai mangé deux glaces à la vanille mais elles étaient trop sucrées!

a Annick went out yesterday. T / F

b She ate a prawn curry. T / F

c It was mild. T / F

d She drank loads of water. T / F

e She ate some chocolate ice cream. T / F

f Now she's moaning about the ice cream! T / F

● Pupil Book pages 40–41

Aujourd'hui, c'est le _____ . Il est _____ .

Langue et grammaire

Plural nouns using –x

To make some nouns plural, you add an –x instead of an –s:

un gâteau	a cake	des gâteaux	cakes
un château	a castle	des châteaux	castles
un cadeau	a present	des cadeaux	presents

The word *au* follows a similar pattern:

*une glace **au** chocolat* a chocolate ice cream
*un gâteau **aux** amandes* an almond cake

Connectives and sequencers

To build longer sentences and express yourself fluently, make good use of connectives and sequencers:

et	and
mais	but
alors	so
ensuite	then
puis	then
enfin	finally
pour commencer	to start with
pour terminer	to end with

 1 Where are these festive foods enjoyed? Write *France, Tunisie, Canada, Vietnam* or *Nouvelle-Calédonie.*

a

_____

b

_____

c

_____

d

_____

e

_____

2 Decide whether or not to put an –x on the end of these words.

a un sandwich au_ fromage

b des nems au_ crevettes

c un gâteau au_ chocolat

d deux gâteau_ au_ chocolat

e deux gâteau_ au_ amandes

f trois cadeau_

g un château_

h une glace au_ noisettes

3 Write in *au*, *à la*, *à l'* or *aux*.

Pizza
_____ tomate   4,50€
_____ jambon   5,20€
_____ fromage   4,90€

Menu
Nems
_____ crabe   3,70€
_____ crevettes 4,20€
_____ curry   4,10€

Tarte
_____ abricot   4€
_____ pommes   3,50€
_____ chocolat   3€
_____ orange   3,20€

4 In pairs. Use the menu from exercise 3. A asks for one or more of the items. B says what the price is.

Exemple

A Je voudrais…

B Ça fait…€.

5 Draw lines from the characters to the special foods.

Hugo, Montréal   tarte au sirop d'érable

Luyen, Hanoï   gâteau aux amandes

Antoine, Nouvelle-Calédonie   nems aux crevettes

Amal, Tunisie   bougna

Lucas, France   dinde aux marrons

6 Add the sequencers to Lucas's account of his Christmas meal. Use the French for these words, in this order:

> to start with   then   and   but   finally

Miam!

_____, je prépare les fruits de mer. _____, je mange de la dinde _____ je bois de l'eau, _____ je ne bois pas de vin. _____, je mange un gâteau aux noisettes.

7 Put Lucas's text from exercise 6 into the perfect tense. ⭐

Pour commencer, j'ai préparé _____

_____

_____

_____

_____

_____

8 Invent some inappropriate festive dishes with horrible ingredients.

J'adore la pizza à l'orange. _____

_____

_____

_____

_____

_____

- Pupil Book pages 42–43

Aujourd'hui, c'est le _____ . Il est _____ .

Langue et grammaire

Following recipes

French recipes generally use verbs in the imperative:

mettez	put	*versez*	pour
ajoutez	add	*mélangez*	mix

Remember that expressions of quantity are followed by *de*:

*250 grammes **de** farine*	250 grams of flour
*une pincée **de** sel*	a pinch of salt
*deux cuillerées **de** sucre*	two spoonfuls of sugar

Remember that *plus de* can be used with a noun or an adverb to mean 'more', and *moins de* is used to mean 'less':

| *plus de sucre* | more sugar |
| *moins de lait* | less milk |

Il faut

The phrase *il faut* literally means 'it is necessary'. It is used very often in French to mean 'you have to' or 'you need':

| *Il faut laisser reposer la pâte.* | You have to let the mixture rest. |
| *Il faut 300 grammes de farine.* | You need 300 grams of flour. |

1 Write the correct number in figures next to each word.

soixante-dix-sept _____   soixante et un _____

quatre-vingt-douze _____   cent trois _____

trois cents _____   soixante et onze _____

quatre-vingt-trois _____   quatre-vingt-treize _____

quatre-vingt-un _____   soixante-dix-neuf _____

2 Now do it the other way round. Write the correct word next to the figure.

95 _____

106 _____

76 _____

66 _____

82 _____

99 _____

115 _____

68 _____

3 Copy the correct words from the box below.

la recette   la poêle   une pincée   l'huile   le beurre   la pâte   une cuillerée   la farine

a

_____

b

_____

c

_____

d

_____

e

_____

f

_____

g

_____

h

_____

4 Put this recipe in the right order. Write 1–9 in the boxes. To help you, here's what you do in English: start with flour, add eggs, add milk, add butter, add salt, mix, put in a pan, fry both sides and serve.

Galettes au fromage

Mélangez bien.

Ajoutez les œufs.

Mettez la farine dans un bol.

Versez la pâte dans une poêle.

Versez le lait dans la pâte.

Ajoutez le beurre.

Servez avec du fromage.

Ajoutez le sel.

Faites cuire des deux côtés.

5 In pairs. Test your partner's comprehension of numbers. Write down ten numbers between 60 and 300. Say them out loud. Your partner notes them down. Then compare. Has your partner got them all right? Then swap roles.

6 Complete these instructions for making guacamole.

Coup____ les avocats.

Vers____ la crème fraîche dans un bol.

Ajout____ les avocats et les épices.

Mélang____ bien.

Mett____ la pâte sur une assiette.

Serv____ avec des fajitas.

7 Why was this cookery attempt so disastrous? List three things that went wrong in as much detail as you can. ⭐

> J'ai essayé de faire des crêpes mais ça a été un désastre. J'ai cassé les oeufs, mais sur le tapis, pas dans un bol. Puis j'ai versé le lait, mais sur mon t-shirt, pas dans la pâte. J'ai fait cuire les crêpes, mais la poêle était trop chaude. Les crêpes étaient noires! Je ne les ai pas servies.

_____

_____

_____

_____

_____

8 In pairs. Write a simple recipe of your own, with each instruction on a separate strip of paper. Use the imperative form of verbs (ending in –ez), as in exercise 5. Give the strips to your partner to sort into the correct order. Can you sort your partner's recipe? ⭐

_____

_____

_____

_____

_____

• Pupil Book pages 56–57

Aujourd'hui, c'est le _____ . Il est 🕐 _____ .

Langue et grammaire

Adjectives that come before the noun

You know that adjectives usually come after the noun they are describing, for example *les yeux verts*. However, some very common adjectives come before the noun, for example:

Elle a une petite bouche. She has a small mouth.
Il a un gros ventre.   He has a fat stomach.

Using the imperfect tense

The imperfect tense can be used to describe someone in the past. You've already learned how to use *c'était* to say what something was like. Now look at the verb *avoir* (to have) in the imperfect tense:

j'avais   I had
tu avais   you had
il/elle/on avait   he/she/we had

Use *avoir* in this tense to describe what someone or something had in the past. For example:
Il avait les yeux verts.   He had green eyes.

Using the correct form of an adjective

Remember to think hard about which form of an adjective you need to use. First check if the noun you are describing is masculine or feminine, and then ask yourself whether it is singular or plural. For example:

a small hand
a hand = *une main* (feminine, singular)
small = *petit* (m), *petite* (f)
= une petite main

small hands
hands = *des mains* (feminine, plural)
small plural = *petits* (m), *petites* (f)
= de petites mains

 Circle the correct ending for each sentence.

a   b   c   d   e

a Gérard Depardieu a **un long nez** / **un nez long**.

b Camille Muffat a **de longues bras** / **de bras longues**.

c Olivier Giroud a **de longues jambes** / **de jambes longues**.

d Anggun a **une bouche grande** / **une grande bouche**.

e Marion Cotillard a **de grands yeux** / **de yeux grands**.

2 Insert the correct form of the adjective.

a Adjective: petit

un _____ nez, une _____ main, de _____ yeux

b Adjective: long

un _____ nez, de _____ jambes

c Adjective: grand

une _____ bouche, un _____ visage, de _____ oreilles

masculine singular: grand, long, petit	**masculine:**	nez, visage
feminine singular: grande, longue, petite	**feminine:**	bouche, jambe, main
masculine plural: grands, longs, petits	**masculine plural:**	yeux
feminine plural: grandes, longues, petites	**feminine plural:**	oreilles

3 Rewrite these sentences in the imperfect (past) tense.

a Claire a les yeux bleus.

_____

b Marc a un gros ventre.

_____

c J'ai de petites mains.

_____

d Tu as de grands pieds.

_____

e Denise a un très long nez.

_____

f Tu as une petite bouche.

_____

g Le prof a de grandes oreilles.

_____

h J'ai de longues jambes.

_____

4 Translate sentences a–d of exercise 3 into English as they were **before** you changed them (i.e. in the present tense).

_____

_____

_____

_____

5 Translate sentences e–h of exercise 3 into English as they are **after** you changed them (i.e. in the imperfect tense).

_____

_____

_____

_____

6 Draw a picture of this person. Exaggerate if you want!

> Aline a de grands yeux, une petite bouche et aussi de petites oreilles. Elle a de courtes jambes et de grands pieds.

7 Following the pattern of exercise 6, write a description of this person in French. ★

_____

_____

_____

_____

_____

_____

8 In pairs. Draw a strange-looking person. A describes in French the person in their drawing for B to draw. Compare the two pictures: are they the same? Then swap roles. ★

3 Topic 2 Entre nous

• Pupil Book pages 58–59

Aujourd'hui, c'est le _____ . Il est _____ .

Langue et grammaire

Reflexive verbs

You know quite a few reflexive verbs, for example: *s'appeler*, *se lever*. Look again at the reflexive pronouns that you use for each part of the verb *se lever* (to get up):

je me lève	*nous nous levons*
tu te lèves	*vous vous levez*
il/elle/on se lève	*ils/elles se lèvent*

When you're using a reflexive verb in a negative sentence the reflexive pronoun and the verb remain together. The two words which form the negative (*ne… pas*, *ne… jamais*, etc.) go around the reflexive pronoun and the verb.

Je ne me lève pas.
Nous ne nous levons pas.
Ils ne se lèvent pas.

Disjunctive pronouns

A disjunctive pronoun is used after certain prepositions, such as *avec* (with) and *à* (to).

Tu peux venir avec moi.	You can come with me.
Je veux aller avec toi.	I want to go with you.
Je m'entends bien avec lui.	I get on well with him.
Il s'entend bien avec elle.	He gets on well with her.

They can also be used for emphasis:

Moi, je suis choqué.	Me, I'm shocked.

Pronunciation

Remember that some adjectives are pronounced differently in their masculine and feminine forms, for example *furieux* and *furieuse*.

---

1 Decide whether these adjectives are in their masculine or feminine form. Write M or F.

déçu	☐	furieux	☐	créative	☐
irritée	☐	choqué	☐	irrité	☐
furieuse	☐	déçue	☐	créatif	☐
ravie	☐	choquée	☐	généreux	☐

2 Choose an adjective from the list below to fit each of these descriptions.

> égoïste   généreuse   furieuse   épuisé   ravi   créative

a A woman who gives all her money to charity. _____

b A man who's just run the Paris marathon. _____

c A boy who only thinks of himself. _____

d A girl who can sing and paint. _____

e A woman who is very angry. _____

f A boy who's just won a gymnastics competition. _____

3 Complete each sentence with the correct form of the adjective.

a   Il est fi _____.

b   Elle est ép _____.

c   Elle est fr _____.

d   Il est ir _____.

e   Il est d _____.

f   Elle est ch _____.

g   Il est r _____.

h   Elle est fu _____.

4 Have some fun! Take turns with a partner to act out some of the adjectives you have learned using mime and facial expressions. Remember to use the feminine form of the adjective if you are a girl talking about yourself or if your partner is a girl.

Example

A acts out 'furieux'

B Tu es frustré?

A Non.

B Tu es furieux?

A Oui! Je suis furieux.

5 Write in the correct disjunctive pronoun.

me = moi   you = toi   him = lui   her = elle

a   J'aime bien mon frère. Je m'entends bien avec _____. *(him)*

b   Tu viens avec _____? *(me)*

c   Je ne veux pas aller avec _____. *(you)*

d   Je n'aime pas ma sœur. Je ne m'entends pas bien avec _____. *(her)*

e   Tu veux danser avec _____? *(me)*

f   Je ne veux pas danser avec _____. *(you)*

6 Write in the correct reflexive pronoun.

a   Je _____ lève à sept heures.   b   Tu ne _____ entends pas bien avec ta sœur.

c   Elle _____ énerve tous les jours.   d   Nous ne _____ disputons jamais.

e   Vous _____ levez à neuf heures?   f   Ils _____ disputent souvent.

Read this problem letter and fill in the gaps.

Les sœurs qui se disputent

Chère Adèle,

J'ai un problème avec ma sœur. Elle est très autoritaire avec moi et je pense qu'elle est aussi égoïste. Nous ne nous entendons pas du tout. Nous nous disputons très souvent. Moi, je suis très déçue parce qu'en général, j'adore ma famille.
Amicalement,

Nadine

a Nadine's sister is _____ and _____.   b They don't _____.

c They often _____.   d Nadine feels _____.

e This is because _____

_____.

 Now translate the whole of the letter in exercise 7 into English. ⭐

_____

_____

_____

_____

Use what you have learned in this topic to write a few sentences in French about a member of your family and how you get on.

_____

_____

_____

_____

• Pupil Book pages 60–61

Aujourd'hui, c'est le [_____]. Il est 🕐 _____.

Langue et grammaire

Using comparatives – a reminder

Use comparatives to compare things, e.g. to say that something is bigger, smaller, more interesting or less beautiful. To form a comparative you use *plus* or *moins* before an adjective.

plus froid	colder
plus beau	more beautiful
moins chaud	less hot
moins important	less important

Using superlatives

Use superlatives when you want to say something is the best, the biggest, the most beautiful, and so on. You form a superlative like this:
definite article (*le*, *la*, or *les*) + *plus/moins* + adjective

Here are some examples:
the prettiest
le plus joli / la plus jolie / les plus jolis / les plus jolies
the least interesting
le moins intéressant / la moins intéressante / les moins intéressants / les moins intéressantes
the most intelligent boy/girl/children
le garçon le plus intelligent / la fille la plus intelligente / les enfants les plus intelligents

Pronunciation

Make sure you pronounce cognates and near cognates correctly. Some are pronounced similarly to English, for example *la baie* but some are different, such as *le climat* and *un glacier*.

1 All these words about natural surroundings are similar to English words, but they may not sound the same. Working in pairs, read them out loud and get your partner to assess how well you have pronounced them. Then swap roles.

un typhon	humide	un glacier	une zone	une dune	le climat	une baie	la mousson

2 Choose words from exercise 1 to solve the clues. What is the mystery word in the tinted boxes down?

a Wet ⬜⬜⬜⬜⬜⬜

b A season of tropical rain ⬜⬜⬜⬜⬜⬜⬜

c A type of tropical storm ⬜⬜⬜⬜⬜⬜

d A mass of ice ⬜⬜⬜⬜⬜⬜⬜

The mystery word = _____

3 Complete the superlative expressions.

> haut(e)(s)   fascinant(e)(s)   beau(x)/belle(s)   intelligent(e)(s)   intéressant(e)(s)

a The most interesting place: L'endroit _____

b The most fascinating castle: Le château _____

c The most beautiful town: La ville _____

d The highest mountain: La montagne _____

e The most intelligent children: Les enfants _____

4 Write *vrai* (true) or *faux* (false).

> Ici en Martinique, nous avons un climat assez varié. En été, il fait très chaud et il y a beaucoup de soleil. Il fait souvent très humide. Mais pendant la saison des ouragans, il y a des orages. Il pleut beaucoup et il fait un vent épouvantable. Pendant cette saison, on reste à la maison. Mais en général, c'est un climat très agréable. Il ne fait jamais froid.

a Il fait froid en hiver en Martinique. _____

b Il ne pleut jamais. _____

c Normalement, il fait chaud. _____

d La saison des ouragans est très agréable. _____

e Il y a beaucoup de soleil en été. _____

f Le climat est varié. _____

5 Using the text in exercise 4 as a stimulus, write a short paragraph about the climate of the country you live in.

Exemple
Ici en..., nous avons...
En été, il fait...

_____

_____

_____

_____

6 Find the French for these expressions in the text and copy them out.

> À mon avis, l'endroit le plus impressionnant et le plus intéressant en France, c'est le Mont St-Michel, en Normandie. Je pense que c'est l'attraction la plus connue et la plus historique de France.

a the best-known attraction   _____

b the most impressive place   _____

c the most historic attraction   _____

d the most interesting place   _____

7 Think of a famous place in your country. Write a couple of sentences about it, remembering to use some superlatives. ⭐

> le/la ... le/la plus intéressant(e)   le/la ... le/la plus impressionnant(e)
> le/la ... le/la plus connu(e)   le/la ... le/la plus historique

_____

_____

8 Use a book of records or the internet to find out three interesting facts about the biggest, smallest, hottest, longest, etc. things in the world.

_____

_____

_____

• Pupil Book pages 62–63

Aujourd'hui, c'est le _____ . Il est _____ .

Langue et grammaire

Using the imperative to give advice

You've already seen how you can use the imperative to give advice or orders to a group of people. Remember that one way of doing this is to use the *vous* form of a verb without the personal pronoun. For example:

Partez immédiatement.   Leave immediately.
Venez tout de suite.   Come straight away.

You can combine use of the imperative with the comparatives that you learned in the previous topic to give detailed instructions:

Allez plus vite.   Go faster.
Allez moins vite.   Slow down.

If the verb is a reflexive verb, for example *se lever*, you must still include the reflexive pronoun:

Levez-vous plus tôt.   Get up earlier.
Couchez-vous plus tôt.   Go to bed earlier.

 1 Draw lines to link the pictures to the words.

 une inondation

 un tremblement de terre

 un incendie de forêt

 un ouragan

 une vague

 un tsunami

une avalanche

2 Now find the underlined words from exercise 1 in this wordsearch and circle them.

t	r	e	m	b	l	e	m	e	n	t
s	f	o	u	r	a	m	i	c	e	o
u	n	s	v	a	g	u	e	y	l	u
n	k	a	n	t	d	v	i	c	j	r
a	v	a	l	a	n	c	h	e	p	a
m	h	c	c	r	p	l	q	n	z	g
i	n	c	e	n	d	i	e	r	o	a
t	r	e	m	t	s	u	b	m	g	n
a	i	n	o	n	d	a	t	i	o	n

3 All these sentences are instructions. Complete them with the correct form of the verb in brackets (ending in –ez).

a _____ dans la maison. (rester)

b _____ les portes fermées. (garder)

c _____ les fenêtres. (fermer)

d N' _____ pas. (hésiter)

e Ne _____ pas de votre chambre. (sortir)

f _____ beaucoup d'eau. (boire)

g N' _____ pas à l'extérieur. (aller)

h _____ votre portable. (utiliser)

4 Translate these instructions into English.

a allez _____   b restez _____

c attrapez _____   d écoutez _____

e hésitez _____   f rappelez-vous _____

g quittez _____   h rentrez _____

5 In pairs. A reads out the commands in exercise 4 in random order. B notes down in English what they have been told to do. Compare notes. Then swap roles.

6 Decide whether you need to add -vous to these commands.

a Quittez _____ la maison.   b Levez _____ de bonne heure.

c Gardez _____ la bouche fermée.   d Lisez _____ les instructions.

e Couchez _____ à onze heures.   f Lavez _____ avant de nager dans la piscine.

g Restez _____ assis.   h Fermez _____ les portes.

reflexive verbs: se coucher   se lever   se laver
non-reflexive verbs: fermer   garder   lire   quitter   rester

7 Read the text and answer the questions. ⭐

Pendant les vacances d'été, on a fait du camping. Un jour, un idiot a laissé tomber une cigarette dans la forêt. Un incendie épouvantable a commencé tout de suite. On a essayé de verser de l'eau sur les flammes mais sans succès.
Le gardien du camping a donné des instructions: 'Laissez vos tentes! Quittez le terrain immédiatement! Montez dans votre voiture et fermez les fenêtres! Sortez de la forêt aussi vite que possible!'

On est rentrés à la maison. Nous avons perdu toutes nos affaires de camping. Mais heureusement les pompiers ont éteint l'incendie en deux heures.

a When did this happen? _____

b Where? _____

c What caused it? _____

d What did they try to do? _____

e What five commands were given? _____

_____ _____

_____ _____

f Where did they go? _____

g What was the unfortunate consequence? _____

h What happened in the end? _____

8 Copy out the five French commands in exercise 7. Then change some of the words to make sentences with new meanings.

_____

_____

_____

_____

_____

• Pupil Book pages 64–65

Aujourd'hui, c'est le [calendar] _____ . Il est [clock] _____ .

Langue et grammaire

The imperfect tense

The imperfect tense is used to describe a past situation or to talk about what you used to do in the past. You form it like this:

1 Take the *nous* form of the present tense, e.g. *habitons*
2 Remove *–ons* so you are left with the stem, e.g. *habit–*
3 Finally, add one of the following endings:

je	–ais	nous	–ions
tu	–ais	vous	–iez
il/elle/on	–ait	ils/elles	–aient

Look at these examples:
J'habitais au Vietnam.   I used to live in Vietnam.
Léa habitait à Montréal. Léa used to live in Montreal.
Nous habitions à Dakar. We used to live in Dakar.
Ils habitaient en Italie.   They used to live in Italy.

Être and avoir in the imperfect tense

You have already met the expression *c'était*. As you can see, the stem for the verb *être* is not formed in the usual way. The stem for *être* in the imperfect tense is *ét–*. Look at this example:
Quand j'étais jeune, j'habitais en France.
When I was young, I used to live in France.

You will also often come across the imperfect form of *avoir*, especially in the phrases *il y avait* (there was/were) and *il n'y avait pas* (there wasn't/weren't).

Pronunciation

Listen carefully to how the imperfect verb endings are pronounced. Can you hear the difference between the *–é* and the *–ais* in *étais*?

1 Add the correct imperfect endings to the verb *habiter*.

Present	**Imperfect**
j'habite	j'habit _____
tu habites	tu habit _____
il/elle/on habite	il/elle/on habit _____
nous habitons	nous habit _____
vous habitez	vous habit _____
ils/elles habitent	ils/elles habit _____

2 Identify whether these sentences are in the present or imperfect tense. Write *P* or *I*.

a Il y a une église dans notre village. _____
b J'habitais à Montpellier. _____
c J'étais malade. _____
d Nous habitons à La Rochelle. _____
e Il y avait un château. _____
f C'était excellent. _____
g Émilie habitait à Dijon. _____
h Maman est en ville. _____

3 Answer the questions with a name.

Maintenant je suis pauvre, mais quand j'étais jeune, j'avais beaucoup d'argent.

Maintenant j'habite dans un petit appartement, mais quand j'étais jeune, j'habitais dans une grande maison.

Maintenant je suis seule, mais quand j'étais jeune, j'avais beaucoup de copines.

Maintenant j'ai un portable, mais quand j'étais jeune, je n'avais pas de téléphone.

M. Letort

Mme Martin

M. Moreau

Mme Pascal

a Who's lonely? _____

b Who uses a mobile? _____

c Who used to be rich? _____

d Who used to have a big house? _____

e Who is poor? _____

f Who didn't have a phone? _____

g Who lives in a little flat? _____

h Who used to have lots of friends? _____

4 Re-read exercise 3 and circle all the imperfect tense verbs.

5 In pairs. A describes to B the place where they used to live when they were younger. Then swap roles.

Exemple

Quand j'étais petit(e), j'habitais… Il y avait… / Il n'y avait pas… C'était…

6 Draw lines to join up these sentences about the disadvantages of living in the country.

a Comme il n'y a pas de fast-food ici,   il faut aller en ville pour danser.

b Comme il n'y a pas d'autobus ici,   il faut aller à l'école en voiture.

c Comme il n'y a pas de discothèque ici,   il est impossible de prendre le train.

d Comme il n'y a pas de café ici,   il faut aller à pied.

e Comme il n'y a pas de collège ici,   il faut aller en ville pour manger un hamburger.

f Comme il n'y a pas de gare ici,   il faut aller en ville pour boire un thé.

7 Translate into French. ⭐

a   I used to live in England.   _____

b   There used to be a bakery.   _____

c   We had a car.   _____

d   Pierre was happy.   _____

e   Marielle lived in France.   _____

f   There weren't many children.   _____

8 Add the imperfect endings to these verbs. ⭐

a Je regard ___ la télé.

b Elle all ___ en ville.

c Il dans ___ chaque soir.

d Nous jou ___ au minigolf.

e J'écout ___ de la musique.

f Ils achet ___ une baguette tous les jours.

• Pupil Book pages 66–67

Aujourd'hui, c'est le _____ . Il est _____ .

Langue et grammaire

The imperfect tense

Here are some more verbs in the imperfect tense. Look at Topic 5 to remind yourself of how they are formed.

infinitive	present tense *nous* form	stem for imperfect tense
faire	nous faisons	fais–
manger	nous mangeons	mange–

Remember to use these verb endings:

je	–ais	nous	–ions
tu	–ais	vous	–iez
il/elle/on	–ait	ils/elles	–aient

Je faisais de la gym.	I used to do gymnastics.
Il mangeait plus de légumes.	He used to eat more vegetables.

When you are using a reflexive verb, don't forget the reflexive pronoun:

*je **me** levais*	*nous **nous** levions*
*tu **te** levais*	*vous **vous** leviez*
*il/elle/on **se** levait*	*ils/elles **se** levaient*

1 Put these phrases into the imperfect tense.

a elle écoute _____

b je joue _____

c il va _____

d nous faisons _____

e on mange _____

f elles se couchent _____

g je rentre _____

h il se lève _____

2 Now complete the sentences in exercise 1 in any way you like. You can use your imagination and add details.

Elle écoutait de la musique classique. _____

_____

_____

_____

_____

_____

_____

_____

3 Select the right options.

Pendant les vacances, c'était génial. Je me levais à dix heures et je mangeais le petit déjeuner à dix heures et demie. Nous allions à la plage tous les après-midi et nous jouions au volley en famille. Tous les soirs, j'allais au resto et je faisais du karaoké. Je chantais très mal, c'était affreux! Je me couchais à minuit. J'adore les vacances!

a   Olivier got up at **10:00 / 10:30**.

b   He ate breakfast at **10:00 / 10:30**.

c   They went to the beach every **morning / afternoon**.

d   They played **volleyball / football**.

e   In the evenings, Olivier **stayed in / went out to eat**.

f   The karaoke sessions were **great / awful**.

g   He went to bed **late / early**.

h   He **enjoyed / didn't enjoy** the holidays.

4 Explain why Olivier's text in exercise 3 is written in the imperfect tense, rather than the perfect tense.

_____

_____

5 Find and copy out the only sentence in exercise 3 that is in the present tense.

_____

_____

6 Draw lines to link the sentence halves.

a Il n'y avait pas d'e-mail,   donc on faisait le vélo.

b Il n'y avait pas de jeux vidéo,   donc on jouait dans le jardin.

c Il n'y avait pas de centre sportif,   donc je partageais ma chambre avec mon frère.

d Je n'avais pas beaucoup d'argent, donc on écrivait des lettres.

e Il n'y avait pas beaucoup de voitures, donc on lisait.

f Notre maison était petite,   donc je n'achetais rien.

7 Take turns with a partner to choose one of these present tense verbs and read it out. The other partner responds as quickly as possible with the imperfect tense version. ⭐

| je mange   je me lève   je fais   je me couche   je joue |

Je mangeais beaucoup de céréales.

_____

_____

_____

_____

_____

8 Now take the six verbs in exercise 7 and turn them into sentences, using the imperfect tense. ⭐

9 Write the sentences from exercise 8 out again, using the *il* form and then the *nous* form. Use separate paper. ⭐

• Pupil Book pages 80–81

Aujourd'hui, c'est le _____ . Il est _____ .

Langue et grammaire

Faire

When talking about what sport you and other people practise, you often need the verb *faire* (to do).
Here is a reminder of the present tense of *faire*:

je fais	nous faisons
tu fais	vous faites
il/elle/on fait	ils/elles font

To refer to a completed action in the past, use the perfect tense:

j'ai fait	nous avons fait
tu as fait	vous avez fait
il/elle/on a fait	ils/elles ont fait

To talk about the future, use the following forms:

je ferai	nous ferons
tu feras	vous ferez
il/elle/on fera	ils/elles feront

Expressions of time

Expressions of time indicate when an action is taking place. Adjectives such as *dernier* (last) and *prochain* (next) need to agree with the noun they go with.

masculine	feminine
l'été dernier	l'année dernière
last summer	last year
le mois prochain	la semaine prochaine
next month	next week

Pronunciation

Don't forget that adding an *e* to the end of a word to make it feminine may change its pronunciation. For example, *prochain* and *prochaine*.

---

 1 Solve the anagrams to find the words for sports and activities. Write in the correct article (*le/la/l'*).

a _____ (LOVYLE)

b _____ (VRNAOI)

c _____ (GIGOGNJ)

d _____ (CATEAORBI)

e _____ (BLAOTOFL)

f _____ (UINOTALCMSU)

g _____ (ANNOITAT)

h   _____ (ISK)

2 Change these forms of *faire*, first into the perfect tense and then into the future.

Present	Perfect	Future
a il fait	_____	_____
b nous faisons	_____	_____
c tu fais	_____	_____
d je fais	_____	_____
e vous faites	_____	_____
f elles font	_____	_____

3 In pairs. A reads out expressions from exercise 2 in random order. B must immediately say 'present', 'perfect' or 'future'. Then swap roles.

4 Complete the expressions of time.

a l'été _____ *(last)*

b la semaine _____ *(next)*

c l'année _____ *(next)*

d le mois _____ *(last)*

e le week-end _____ *(last)*

f l'été _____ *(next)*

g la semaine _____ *(last)*

h l'hiver _____ *(last)*

5 Read Aline's account and identify the verbs in the following ways:

- Draw a line under present tense verbs.

- Draw a dotted line under perfect tense verbs.

- Draw a wiggly line under future tense verbs.

- Circle the expressions of time.

> Moi, j'aime faire du jogging. Hier, je suis allée à la campagne et j'ai fait cinq kilomètres à pied. Je fais aussi de la natation, mais pas tous les jours.
> La semaine prochaine, j'irai en ville et je ferai de la natation à la piscine municipale. Mon frère Pascal n'est pas sportif. Il joue au foot de temps en temps et demain il fera du judo après l'école.

Aline

6 Are these statements true or false? Circle T or F.

a Aline is sporty. T / F

b Tomorrow she'll run 5 kilometres. T / F

c Pascal is her brother. T / F

d He's going swimming tomorrow. T / F

e Aline went jogging yesterday. T / F

f Pascal is planning to do some judo. T / F

g Aline goes swimming every day. T / F

h The swimming pool is in town. T / F

7 In pairs. A asks these questions about sport. B answers. Then swap roles. Your answers don't have to be true! ⭐

• Qu'est-ce que tu fais aujourd'hui?

• Qu'est-ce que tu as fait hier?

• Qu'est-ce que tu feras demain?

8 Translate the text in exercise 5 into English, starting with *Mon frère Pascal...*

_____

_____

_____

_____

9 Using exercise 5 as a model, write a short paragraph about sport. ⭐
Mention:

• what you do

• what you have done

• what you will do.

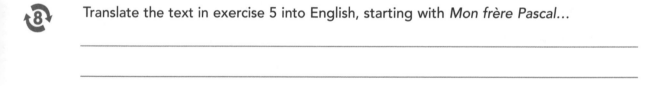

je ferai	I will do
j'irai	I will go
ce sera	it will be

_____

_____

_____

• Pupil Book pages 82–83

Aujourd'hui, c'est le _____ . Il est _____ .

Langue et grammaire

The perfect tense

You already know how to make simple forms of the perfect tense, using the present tense of *avoir* with the past participle of the verb you want to use.

J'ai sauté.	I jumped.
Il a escaladé.	He climbed.
Elle a couru.	She ran.

You also know that *aller* makes its perfect tense with the present tense of *être* rather than *avoir*.

Je suis allé(e)   I went

Pronunciation

Remember that these past participles are pronounced the same way, even if you have added an *e* or an *s*. The extra letters are silent.

There are other verbs like *aller* that make their perfect tense with *être*. Here are those you will meet in this topic.

aller	to go	*je suis allé(e)*
venir	to come	*tu es venu(e)*
partir	to leave	*il est parti*
arriver	to arrive	*elle est arrivée*
rester	to stay	*on est resté(e)s*
rentrer	to go home	*ils sont rentrés*
retourner	to go back	*elles sont retournées*

With these verbs, the past participle agrees with the **subject**. This means you need to add an *e* if the subject is feminine, an *s* if it is plural, and *es* if it is feminine plural. For example, the past participle in *je suis allé(e)* is spelled *allé* (if the speaker is masculine) or *allée* (if the speaker is feminine).

 1 Complete the sentences with either *avoir* or *être* in the present tense.

a Il _____ sauté.

b On _____ allés au parc.

c Manon _____ couru trois kilomètres.

d Abdou _____ arrivé à cinq heures.

e Sophie _____ restée à la maison.

f Pierre _____ escaladé le mur.

g Nous _____ rentrés à six heures.

h Elles _____ allées à Paris.

 2 Which sentence in exercise 1 refers to which picture? Write a–h.

 _____    _____   _____   _____

 _____   _____   _____   _____

3   Decide whether to add *–e*, *–s* or *–es* to the past participle, or leave it as it is. If you want to leave it as it is, draw a dash (–).

a Elles sont retourné _____.

b Mélanie est parti _____.

c Luc est venu _____.

d Romain: 'Je suis rentré _____.'

e Clémence: 'Je suis rentré _____.'

f Clémence et Romain: 'Nous sommes arrivé _____.'

g Clémence et Mélanie: 'Nous sommes arrivé _____.'

h Roger et Thomas: 'Nous sommes parti _____.'

4 In pairs. A reads out one of the present tense phrases below (a–f). B immediately puts it into the perfect tense. Then swap roles.

Exemple

A je vais

B je suis allé(e)

B nous partons

a il rentre	**b** elle saute	**c** vous courez
d j'arrive	**e** tu rentres	**f** nous partons

5   Put the activities in the right order according to the text. Write 1, 2, 3, etc.

Randonnée en vélo

Mes parents, ma sœur et moi, nous avons quitté le camping et nous avons traversé le pont. Nous sommes passés devant la mairie et nous sommes arrivés au café vers midi. On a bu une limonade et ensuite mes parents sont restés au café et ma sœur et moi, nous sommes retournés au camping, où on a joué aux boules.

a having a drink _____

b going back to the campsite _____

c crossing a bridge _____

d arriving at a café _____

e playing boules _____

f staying at the café _____

g leaving a campsite _____

h going past a town hall _____

6 Translate these expressions into French.

a I (female) went   _____

b Hugo left   _____

c We (two females) left   _____

d We (two males) stayed   _____

e She jumped   _____

f They (two males) arrived   _____

g They (two females) arrived   _____

h Sophie ran   _____

7 Translate the text in exercise 5 into English from *Mes parents...* to *...midi.* ⭐

_____

_____

_____

_____

_____

8 Write a short account of a trip into town. Be adventurous and add as much extra detail as you can. ⭐
Include this information:

• Ali and his sister Fatima went by bus.

• Together they went swimming.

• Ali went rollerblading.

• Fatima stayed in a café.

• Together they returned home.

> Fatima / Ali / Elle / Il est... / a ...
>
> Fatima et Ali / Ils sont... / ont...

_____

_____

_____

_____

_____

• Pupil Book pages 84–85

Aujourd'hui, c'est le _____ . Il est _____ .

Langue et grammaire

Giving locations – a reminder

Use *à* to introduce the name of a town, village or city:
C'était à Rio de Janeiro.   It was in Rio de Janeiro.

Use *en* to introduce the name of a feminine country:
Beijing est en Chine.   Beijing is in China.

Use *au* with the name of a masculine country:
Vancouver est au Canada.   Vancouver is in Canada.

Use *aux* when the country has a plural name:
Salt Lake City est aux   Salt Lake City is in the
  États-Unis.   United States.

Giving dates

When saying the year, always start with *deux mille* (never with *vingt*):

2001	*deux mille un*	2011	*deux mille onze*
2010	*deux mille dix*	2016	*deux mille seize*

Pronunciation

You might think that if the name of a place is spelled the same, or nearly the same, in French as in English, it will be pronounced the same way. Be careful! That is not always the case. For example, *Turin*, *Athènes* and *Brésil*.

1 Write these dates in figures.

a deux mille cinq _____

b deux mille quinze _____

c deux mille vingt-deux _____

d deux mille deux _____

e deux mille douze _____

f deux mille trente _____

2 Now write these dates in words.

a 2001 _____

b 2011 _____

c 2014 _____

d 2004 _____

e 2040 _____

f 2025 _____

3 Draw lines to link the French and English expressions.

j'aime bouger   the UK

les JO   I love climbing

je suis gâté   in which country

j'adore l'escalade   I like surfing

dans quel pays   it was great

j'aime faire du surf   I like being active

c'était génial   the Olympic Games

le Royaume-Uni   I'm spoilt

4 Write in à, *au*, *aux* or *en*.

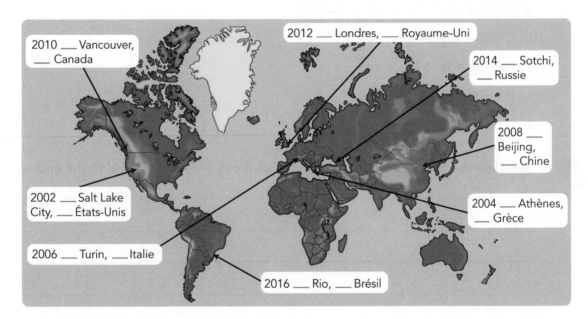

2010 ___ Vancouver, ___ Canada

2012 ___ Londres, ___ Royaume-Uni

2014 ___ Sotchi, ___ Russie

2008 ___ Beijing, ___ Chine

2002 ___ Salt Lake City, ___ États-Unis

2004 ___ Athènes, ___ Grèce

2006 ___ Turin, ___ Italie

2016 ___ Rio, ___ Brésil

5 In pairs. A asks *Tu aimes bouger?* B answers with three types of sport: *J'aime... et j'adore... mais je n'aime pas...* Then swap roles.

6 Answer the questions with 'yes' or 'no'.

> J'adore faire de l'équitation. J'ai un cheval qui s'appelle Hervé. Je suis gâtée parce qu'Hervé est un cheval très sympa, qui est installé dans une ferme près de chez nous. Je fais du cheval tous les week-ends. Pendant les grandes vacances, on a loué des chevaux en Provence, dans le sud de la France. On s'est promenés à cheval sur la plage. C'était génial! L'année prochaine, je voudrais bien faire de l'équitation au Maroc.

a Does Yvonne have her own horse?   _____

b Does she keep it at home?   _____

c Did she buy a horse in Provence?   _____

d Is Provence in the south of France?   _____

e Did she ride on the beach?   _____

f Did she ride in Morocco?   _____

g Is her brother called Hervé?   _____

h Is Hervé nice?   _____

7 Translate the text in exercise 6 into English, from *Je fais du cheval* to the end. ⭐

_____

_____

_____

_____

8 Write a few lines about sports you like and dislike. Try to include reasons and mention some things you **have done** and some things you **would like to do**. ⭐

- Revise perfect and future verb forms.
- Use je voudrais...

- Express opinions using adjectives.
- Use expressions of time.

_____

_____

_____

_____

4 Topic 4 Le Tour de France

• Pupil Book pages 86–87

Aujourd'hui, c'est le _____ . Il est _____ .

Langue et grammaire

High numbers

Use the words *cent* (a hundred), *mille* (a thousand) and *un million* (one million) to construct high numbers:

1000	*mille*
2000	*deux mille*
3000	*trois mille*
1903	*mille neuf cent trois*
2013	*deux mille treize*
2014	*deux mille quatorze*
2015	*deux mille quinze*
3400	*trois mille quatre cents*

When talking about dates, introduce the year with the preposition *en*:

Je suis né en 2002.   I was born in 2002.

Ordinal numbers

You already know that the French for first is *premier/première*. To make the other ordinal numbers, simply add *ième*. For numbers ending in *e*, remove the *e* before adding the ending.

1st	*premier/première*
2nd	*deuxième*
3rd	*troisième*
4th	*quatrième*
100th	*centième*
101st	*cent unième*

Pronunciation

Notice the difference in the pronunciation of *ll* in *maillot/meilleur* compared to *mille/million*.

---

1 Answer this cycling vocabulary quiz. What word do you find and what does it mean?

1 ☐☐☐☐☐☐   1 team

2 ☐☐☐☐☐☐☐   2 jersey

3 ☐☐☐☐☐☐☐   3 winner

4 ☐☐☐☐☐☐☐☐   4 climber

5 ☐☐☐☐☐☐   5 race

The mystery word is _____ and it means _____ .

Answer these multiple-choice questions about the Tour de France.

1 Le Tour de France a commencé en

    a 1953   **b** 2003   **c** 1903

2 La course finit à

    a Bruxelles   **b** Paris   **c** Nantes

3 Il y a combien d'équipes?

    a 29   **b** 20   **c** 22

4 Le Tour a lieu en

    a juillet   **b** juin   **c** août

5 La course dure

    a trois semaines   **b** une semaine   **c** deux semaines

6 Il y a combien de téléspectateurs?

    a 2 millions   **b** 12 millions   **c** 20 millions

Label the pieces of cycling gear. The words are given below to choose from.

casque

gants

chaussettes

maillot

chaussures

short

VÉLOMONDE

In pairs. B thinks of a piece of cycling equipment and A guesses. Then swap roles.

Exemple

A Tu as des gants?   **B** Non.
A Tu as un maillot?   **B** Oui! J'ai un maillot.

Write these numbers in figures.

  a cent   _____   **b** mille   _____

  c deux mille   _____   **d** trois mille cinq cents   _____

  e quatre mille treize _____   **f** six mille trois cents douze _____

6 Write these numbers in words.

a 1100 _____ b 2500 _____ c 4620 _____

7 Write *premier*, *deuxième*, and so on by each name on the leaderboard.

Champion Cycliste

1	David César	38.0
2	John Walker	29.0
3	Freddi Letort	27.5
4	Marc Prévost	23.0
5	Pierre Zander	22.2

8 Write the name of the rider next to each jersey.

En direct du Tour de France aujourd'hui à Avignon, bonjour tout le monde. Alain Dupré n'a que 18 ans mais il fait une très bonne course. Marc Prévost est le meilleur coureur en montagne. Bruno Timbre est le sprinteur le plus rapide, mais le numéro 1 du Tour aujourd'hui, c'est…David César!

a _____

b _____

c _____

d  _____

The yellow jersey is for the overall winner. The dotted jersey is for the best climber. The white jersey is for the best young rider. The green jersey is for the best sprinter.

• Pupil books pages 88–89

Aujourd'hui, c'est le [calendar] _____. Il est [clock] _____.

Langue et grammaire

Past tenses

When describing something that happened in the past, choose between the perfect tense and the imperfect tense.

Use the perfect tense to describe a completed action in the past:

Je suis allé au stade.	I went to the stadium.
Il a regardé un match.	He watched a match.
Mon équipe a gagné.	My team won.

Use the imperfect tense to describe what it was like:

C'était fantastique.	It was fantastic.
Mon frère était fier.	My brother was proud.
Il y avait deux équipes.	There were two teams.

Il y a and Il y avait

You have already come across the phrase _il y a_, meaning 'there is' or 'there are'. The equivalent phrase in the imperfect tense is _il y avait_:

Il y a onze joueurs.	There are eleven players.
Il y avait beaucoup de spectateurs.	There were / used to be a lot of spectators.

Pronunciation

Listen carefully to the word _fauteuil_ and make sure you pronounce it correctly.

---

1 Draw lines to link the words to the sports.

a le hockey sur luge

b le boccia

c le goalball

d le rugby-fauteuil

e le handibasket

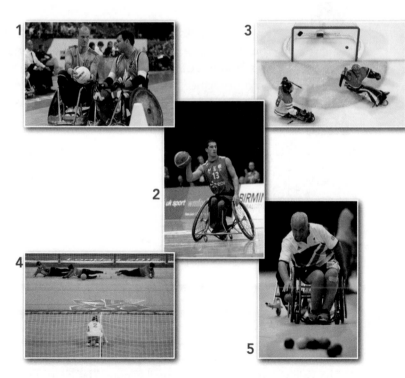

1

3

2

4

5

2 Decide whether these are Olympic or Paralympic sports. Write 'O' or 'P'.

a goalball _____

b handibasket _____

c rugby-fauteuil _____

d hockey sur glace _____

e hockey sur luge _____

f handball _____

g basket _____

3 Draw a straight line under the imperfect tense verbs and a wiggly line under the perfect tense verbs.

> Hier, je suis allé voir un match de rugby. J'y suis allé avec Lucas. C'était au Stade de France. La France jouait contre l'Écosse. C'était passionnant. La France a gagné, heureusement.

_____

_____

_____

_____

_____

4 Now fill in Sophie's reply.

Sophie went with Justine to see a basketball match. It was at the Palais Omnisports de Paris Bercy. France was playing against England. It was very boring and England won.

5 Fill in the missing vocabulary.

> Le goalball est un sport paralympique. Il ressemble au handball mais les _____ (*players*) sont en _____ (*wheelchair*). Il y a trois joueurs par _____ (*team*). On essaye de marquer un _____ (*goal*).

6 Copy the corresponding French expressions from the box below.

> C'était comment?   Tu étais avec qui?   Qui a gagné?
> Qu'est-ce que tu as fait?   C'était où?

a What did you do? _____

b Who were you with? _____

c Where was it? _____

d What was it like? _____

e Who won? _____

7 Have this conversation with a partner. Then swap roles and repeat.

A

Ask what B did yesterday.

Ask who they were with.

Ask where it was.

Ask how it was.

Ask who won.

B

Say you went to a football match.

Give names.

Say where it was.

Give your opinion.

Say who won.

8 Translate into French. ⭐

a I went to the sports centre.

_____

b There was a basketball match.

_____

c There were two teams.

_____

d I watched the match.

_____

e It was excellent.

_____

• Pupil Book pages 90–91

Aujourd'hui, c'est le _____ . Il est _____ .

Langue et grammaire

The future tense

The formal way of talking about the future in French is to use the future tense. To form the future tense of regular verbs, you simply need to add the following endings to the infinitive:

visiter
*je visiter**ai***
*tu visiter**as***
*il/elle/on visiter**a***

An easy way of remembering these endings is to note they are the same as the present tense of *avoir*.
*j'**ai***   *tu **as***   *il/elle/on **a***

Irregular verbs

A number of common verbs have an irregular stem in the future tense but the endings are still the same:

infinitive	stem	future tense
aller	*ir–*	*j'irai, tu iras, il/elle/on ira*
faire	*fer–*	*je ferai, tu feras, il/elle/on fera*
être	*ser–*	*je serai, tu seras, il/elle/on sera*

Note that all forms of the infinitive have the letter *r* just before the endings. If there is no letter *r*, either you have left it out by mistake or it's not the future tense! Make sure you pronounce them correctly. Listen to the examples used in the topic.

Draw lines to link the sentences to places on the map of Martinique.

Ici on peut faire du surf.

C'est une très belle plage.

La montagne Pelée

Saint-Pierre

Tartane

C'est ici qu'habite Emma.

Fort-de-France

Ce volcan est dangereux.

C'est ici qu'on arrive en Martinique.

les Salines

2 Put these verbs into the future tense.

a je vais _____

b il arrive _____

c elle fait _____

d tu visites _____

e on regarde _____

f je suis _____

g elle gagne _____

h il commence _____

i tu joues _____

j on rentre _____

k je finis _____

l elle part _____

3 Three of the future forms in exercise 2 are 'irregular'. Which are they?

_____   _____   _____

4 Unjumble these future tense sentences.

a les bananes Je de plantations visiterai

_____

b à passera Hugo Martinique semaines la deux

_____

c plongée ferai Je la de

_____

d volcan On voir ira le

_____

e arrivera heures Hugo cinq à

_____

f mangroves On canoë-kayak visitera en les

_____

5 In pairs. A says three future tense sentences. B contradicts by changing the information after the verb. Then swap roles.

Exemple

A J'irai à Paris.   **B** J'irai à Londres.

J'irai à Paris.	Le film commencera à 5h.
Je ferai du ski.	Je jouerai aux boules.
Je serai à la plage.	Le match finira à 4h.

6 Read what Emma says and answer the questions below.

What will Hugo do:

a On Tuesday? _____

b On Wednesday? _____

c On Thursday? _____

> Hugo, tu arriveras chez moi lundi. Ça sera génial! Mardi, on passera la journée à la plage. On fera de la voile et de la plongée. Mercredi, on visitera les plantations de bananes et jeudi on visitera les mangroves en canoë-kayak. Ce sera super!

7 Translate into French using the verbs in the box. ⭐

| être | faire | passer | arriver | visiter |

a Hugo will visit the mangroves.

_____

b He will spend three days with Emma.

_____

c He will go sailing.

_____

d He will arrive at 7 o'clock.

_____

e That will be great!

_____

8 Use the prompts to write sentences like the one in the example, using the present and then the future tense. ⭐

a je – être – Marseille – Nice   *Maintenant je suis à Marseille mais demain je serai à Nice.*

b on – regarder – film – télé   _____

c tu – faire – voile – ski   _____

d elle – visiter – église – château   _____

e je – jouer – volley – golf   _____

f on – aller – café – cinéma   _____

• Pupil Book pages 104–105

Aujourd'hui, c'est le _____ . Il est _____ .

Langue et grammaire

Direct and indirect object pronouns

A direct object is the noun (person or thing) in a sentence that the verb is about.
I find **the book** interesting.

An indirect object is the noun (person or thing) in a sentence that the verb is done **to** or **for**:
I'm buying the book for **Abdou**.

Remember, pronouns are used in place of nouns. For example 'it' in place of 'book' and 'him' in place of 'Abdou':
I'm buying **it** for **him**.

In French, direct and indirect object pronouns usually come **before** the verb.

Direct object pronouns

Direct object pronouns are:
• *le* = it (in place of a masculine noun)
• *la* = it (in place of a feminine noun)
• *les* = them (in place of a plural noun)

Je trouve le livre intéressant. Je le trouve intéressant.
Tu aimes mon porte-clés? – Euh, je le trouve curieux.

Je trouve la géographie intéressante. Je la trouve intéressante.
Tu aimes la carte postale? – Oui, je la trouve très jolie.

Je trouve les films intéressants. Je les trouve intéressants.
Tu aimes les musées? – Non, je les trouve ennuyeux.

Indirect object pronouns

• *lui* = him or her
  Je lui achète un cadeau.   I'm buying a present for him/her.
• *leur* = them
  Je leur donne mon adresse.   I'm giving my address to them.

 1 Unjumble the French adjectives. Write the word on the line, and then draw a line to link it to its English translation.

a ehmco   _____   mysterious

b zarbire   _____   strange

c lijo   _____   ridiculous

d yémitsrxue   _____   romantic

e exicruu   _____   sinister

f iérlatse   _____   ugly

g eqoriatunm   _____   pretty

h ieurdicl   _____   realistic

i gdnaoétût   _____   weird

j neisrtis   _____   disgusting

2 Draw lines to match the French words to the pictures.

un aimant

une carte postale

un parapluie

un porte-clés

une règle

un tapis de souris

a

b

c

d

e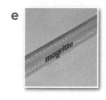

f

3 Rewrite these sentences, replacing the object with a direct object pronoun (*le*, *la* or *les*).

Exemple

Je trouve la chimie intéressante.

Je la trouve intéressante.

a Je trouve la peinture moche.

_____

b Je trouve les cartes postales jolies.

_____

c Je trouve le film sinistre.

_____

d Je trouve le salami dégoûtant.

_____

e Je trouve ce livre romantique.

_____

f Je trouve l'idée (f) ridicule.

_____

g Je trouve le journal réaliste.

_____

h Je trouve ton frère bizarre.

_____

4 Read this conversation. Underline all the direct object pronouns and circle all the indirect object pronouns.

> Tu as trouvé un souvenir pour tes parents?

> Oui, je leur achète ces porte-clés. Je les trouve jolis.

> Et moi, j'achète une carte postale pour mon frère.
> Je lui envoie la carte pour son anniversaire.

> Et tu as trouvé quelque chose pour Justine?

> Oui, je lui donne cette tasse parce que je la trouve amusante.

5 Re-read the conversation in exercise 5 and answer these questions.

a What will Maeva's parents get? _____

b What does she think of them? _____

c Who's getting a postcard? _____

d What's it for? _____

e What will Justine get? _____

f What does Abdou think of it? _____

6 Translate into English. ⭐

a Je la trouve mystérieuse. _____

b Je le trouve dégoûtant. _____

c Je les trouve ridicules. _____

d Il l'aime. _____

e Nous la regardons. _____

f Elle les achète. _____

7 Answer these questions for yourself, using a direct object pronoun instead of the object. ⭐

a Comment tu trouves Lady Gaga?

_____

b Comment tu trouves les Schtroumpfs? (the Smurfs)

_____

c Comment tu trouves les Jeux olympiques?

_____

• Pupil Book pages 106–107

Aujourd'hui, c'est le _____ . Il est _____ .

Langue et grammaire

Colours

Remember that colours go after the noun:
un tee-shirt rose   a pink T-shirt

To say if a colour is dark or light, use _foncé_ or _clair_ after the colour. For example:
bleu clair   light blue
vert foncé   dark green

When used like this the colour word **does not** change to match the gender of the noun
une chemise bleue
une chemise bleu clair (with no extra e on _bleu_ even though _chemise_ is a feminine noun)

It's the same when you use two colours together, for example, blue-green. Notice the hyphen:
une jupe bleu-vert   a blue-green skirt

Making longer sentences

Joining short sentences together will make your language more sophisticated. You already know the connectives _et_ (and) and _mais_ (but) and you'll see some new ones in the _Vocabulaire_ box.

Je n'ai pas assez d'argent. Je ne peux pas acheter la robe.
I don't have enough money. I can't buy the dress.

Comme je n'ai pas assez d'argent je ne peux pas acheter la robe.
As I don't have enough money, I can't buy the dress.

You can also use the relative pronoun _qui_ (who/which):
J'ai un copain. Il s'appelle Hugo.
I have a friend. His name is Hugo.
J'ai un copain qui s'appelle Hugo.
I have a friend whose name is Hugo.

 1 Copy in the colours of the garments.

rose   bleu-vert   vert clair   bleu foncé   noir et blanc   vert foncé   bleu clair   gris

2 Write in the adjectives.

a un tee-shirt _____ (blue)   b un tee-shirt _____ (light blue)

c une chemise _____ (green)   d une chemise _____ (light green)

e une jupe _____ (grey)   f une jupe _____ (dark grey)

3 Underline the connective in each of these sentences.

a Comme j'ai raté le train, je suis arrivé en retard.

b Même s'il pleut demain, on va aller au bord de la mer.

c Le tableau est triste mais je l'aime bien.

d Je prends le bus puisque j'habite à la campagne.

e Je n'aime pas l'œuvre parce que je ne la comprends pas.

f Samedi on va au musée d'art et dimanche on va au centre sportif.

4 Join each pair of sentences to make one longer sentence using *qui*.

a J'ai un cheval. Il s'appelle Hervé.

_____

b Maeva a acheté un tee-shirt. Il est vert foncé.

_____

c Voici une œuvre. Elle s'appelle *Le chat rose*.

_____

d Nous avons une maison. Elle est située à la campagne.

_____

e Paris est une ville. Elle est très grande.

_____

f J'ai vu un tableau. Il était très sombre.

_____

g Banksy est un artiste. Il habite à Londres.

_____

h J'ai un frère. Il est plus âgé que moi.

_____

5 In pairs. A reads out a few pairs of sentences from exercise 4. B connects them, using *qui*. Don't refer to your answers to exercise 4! Then swap roles.

Exemple

A J'ai un cheval. Il s'appelle Hervé.

B J'ai un cheval qui s'appelle Hervé.

6 Find these expressions in the text.

> Voici un exemple de l'art à l'extérieur. C'est une œuvre qui se trouve dans la vieille ville de Marseille. C'est un portrait géant d'un oiseau gris qui tourne la tête à gauche. L'œuvre est bizarre et un peu sinistre mais elle est très connue dans la région.

a very well-known   _____

b turns left   _____

c the old town   _____

d open-air art   _____

e a huge portrait   _____

7 Translate the text in exercise 6 into English, from *C'est un portrait* to the end. ⭐

_____

_____

_____

8 Translate these sentences into French. ⭐

a I think it's strange and a bit boring.

_____

b It's a painting which is very big.

_____

c Because I think the cat is pretty, I like it.

_____

d It's realistic but ugly.

_____

• Pupil Book pages 108–109

Aujourd'hui, c'est le _____ . Il est _____

Langue et grammaire

Irregular past participles

You know that to form the perfect tense of a verb you use the present tense of the verb *avoir* or *être* and the past participle of the verb. For example, *j'ai mangé* or *je suis allé*. The past participles of some verbs are irregular and it's important to learn them. Here are some commonly used verbs that have irregular past participles:

infinitive		past participle
naître	to be born	né(e)
lire	to read	lu
écrire	to write	écrit

Questions

Here are some question words (interrogatives) and examples of how they can be added to a sentence to make a question:
quand (when)   you eat = *tu manges*
When do you eat? = *Tu manges quand?*

où (where)   you are going = *tu vas*
Where are you going? = *Tu vas où?*

quel(le) (which)   you are reading = *tu lis*
Which book are you reading? = *Tu lis quel livre?*

qui (who)   your favourite book = *ton livre préféré*
Who wrote your favourite book? = *Qui a écrit ton livre préféré?*

qu'est-ce que (what)   you are writing = *tu écris*
What are you writing? = *Qu'est-ce que tu écris?*

combien de (how many)   you have dogs = *tu as des chiens*
How many dogs do you have? = *Tu as combien de chiens?*
(note how *des* changes to *de*)

 1 Draw lines to link the French and English question words.

 2 Unjumble these four words from the world of literature. What do they mean?

	Word	Meaning
a cviéinar	_____	_____
b ulelnevo	_____	_____
c namor	_____	_____
d turuae	_____	_____

3 Write in the correct question words.

a Tu es né _____? (when)

b Tu as lu _____ romans? (how many)

c Tu as téléchargé _____ livre? (which)

d _____ as-tu trouvé ce roman? (how)

e _____ tu as lu pendant les vacances? (what)

f _____ as-tu acheté ce livre? (why)

g Tu prends tes vacances _____? (where)

h Tu préfères _____ nouvelle? (which)

4 Write in the correct past participles.

a Maeva a _____ un roman pour les vacances. (downloaded)

b Abdou a _____ un livre puisqu'il n'a pas de tablette. (bought)

c Jules Verne est _____ à Nantes. (born)

d As-tu _____ le nouveau roman de J.K. Rowling? (read)

e Victor Hugo a _____ Les Misérables. (wrote)

5 In pairs. A asks these questions and B answers. Then swap roles.

- Tu es né(e) quand?
- Tu es né(e) où?
- Qu'est-ce que tu fais ce soir?
- Tu manges à quelle heure?
- Tu as combien de livres?

6 Read the text and answer the questions (a–h).

Pour les vacances, j'ai acheté le livre
Les Trois Mousquetaires. C'est un roman
d'Alexandre Dumas, qui est un écrivain français
très célèbre. Il est né à Villers-Cotterêts en 1802
et il a écrit plusieurs livres. La semaine dernière,
j'ai lu *Le Comte de Monte-Cristo*, un autre roman
de Dumas. Dumas a écrit *Les Trois Mousquetaires*
en 1844. C'est l'histoire de quatre amis, Athos,
Porthos, Aramis et D'Artagnan.

a Why did Sophie buy a book? _____

b What is the title (in English)? _____

c Did she download it? _____

d Who was Alexandre Dumas? _____

e Where and when was he born? _____

f Has Sophie read anything else by him? _____

g When did he write *Les Trois Mousquetaires*? _____

h Who or what is it about? _____

7 Translate the first sentence of the exercise 6 text into English.

_____

_____

8 Refer back to exercise 3. Write your own answers to all the questions in that exercise. ⭐

_____

_____

_____

_____

_____

_____

9 Translate these sentences into French. ⭐

a Which book did you download?

_____

b Where was Dumas born?

_____

c When was Dumas born?

_____

d How many books did Dumas write?

_____

e What have you read?

_____

5 Topic 4 Les stars du cinéma français

• Pupil Book pages 110–111

Aujourd'hui, c'est le _____. Il est _____.

Langue et grammaire

Dates
Remember, the way you say a year in French is not the same as the way you say it in English. Look at the differences:

1925   in English you say – nineteen twenty five
in French you say – *mille neuf cent vingt-cinq*

2002   in English you say – two thousand and two
in French you say – *deux mille deux*

Avoir and *être* in the perfect tense
Remember that for most verbs you use *avoir* to form the perfect tense and that you must learn the list of verbs that you have to use *être* with. Look at page 82 for a reminder of verbs that use *être*.

Remember that you also need to use être with:
• Verbs that are derived from the list of *être* verbs. For example *venir* (to come) is in the list and so to form the perfect tense of *devenir* (to become) you also have to use *être*.
• Reflexive verbs. You have to use *être* to form the perfect tense of all reflexive verbs.

Pronunciation
Remember that the rules of pronunciation that you have learned also apply to names. You often do not pronounce the final letter. For example:
Cannes   Yves   Signoret   Allégret   Montand

 1 Choose French verbs from the box to translate these English verbs.

| avoir lieu   devenir   divorcer   gagner   se marier   tomber amoureux |

a to win   _____   **b** to take place _____

c to get married   _____   **d** to become   _____

e to get divorced _____   **f** to fall in love _____

2 Write out these dates in figures.

a deux mille quatorze   _____

b deux mille neuf cent soixante-six   _____

c deux mille quatre-vingt-sept   _____

d deux mille quatre-vingt-dix-sept   _____

e deux mille neuf   _____

f deux mille onze   _____

g mille neuf cent quatre-vingt-dix-neuf   _____

h mille neuf cent cinquante-quatre   _____

3 In pairs. Both write down five years of their choice (in figures) without showing them to their partner. A reads out their dates one by one in French, once only each. B writes down the dates, without asking for a repeat. At the end, compare notes and discuss any misunderstandings. Then swap roles.

4 In pairs. A reads these words aloud. B assesses how well pronounced they are.

Chartres   brevet   Monserrat   Mitterrand   Muscadet

Swap roles. B reads these words aloud.

Tours   cornet   cabaret   Bertrand   Sarlat

5 Write in *ai*, *a*, *ont*, *suis*, *est*, or *sont*.

a Je _____ né(e) en 2001.

b Pascal _____ né en 1999.

c J'_____ grandi à Saint-Malo.

d Mes parents se _____ mariés en 1995.

e Ils _____ divorcé en 2010.

f Moi, je _____ tombée amoureuse de Pascal l'année dernière.

g Pascal _____ joué de la musique pour moi.

h Il _____ gagné mon cœur.

6 Translate sentences d–h from exercise 5 into English.

_____

_____

_____

_____

_____

7 Read the text about Charlotte Gainsbourg. True or false? Circle the appropriate letter.

> Charlotte Gainsbourg est née à Londres en 1971. Elle est la fille de Jane Birkin, l'actrice anglaise, et de Serge Gainsbourg, un chanteur français. Charlotte a travaillé comme actrice et comme chanteuse aussi. Elle a trois enfants avec son partenaire, Yvan Attal. Charlotte a joué dans son premier film, *Paroles et musique* (1984), et dans beaucoup d'autres films. En 2009, Charlotte a enregistré un CD qui s'appelle *IRM*, réalisé avec le musicien Beck.

a	She was born in Paris.	T / F
b	Both her parents were in show business.	T / F
c	They have three children.	T / F
d	She's made lots of films.	T / F
e	She's never recorded an album.	T / F
f	She took part in a film with Beck.	T / F
g	She can sing as well as act.	T / F

8 Translate this paragraph into English.

> Le Festival du film de Berlin est un grand festival de cinéma international. Le premier festival a eu lieu en 1951. Le prix le plus important de ce festival est «L'Ours d'or». C'est le prix pour le meilleur film.

Berlinale Palast

_____

_____

_____

_____

9 Translate into French.

a I was born in Lyon.   _____

b I grew up in Paris.   _____

c I fell in love in 2010.   _____

d I married in 2013.   _____

e I haven't got divorced.   _____

• Pupil Book pages 112–113

Aujourd'hui, c'est le _____ . Il est _____

Langue et grammaire

Agreeing and disagreeing

It's important to be able to agree or disagree with other people's ideas and to express how strongly you feel about things by using a range of expressions. Look at these examples:

Tu veux jouer à la pétanque, Félix?
Ah oui, bonne idée.
Ah oui, d'accord.
Oh non – pas ça, Thomas. C'est ennuyeux!
Tu rigoles!

Making longer sentences

You've seen how to use connectives like *mais* and *comme* to make your writing more sophisticated.

Remember that the relative pronoun *qui* can also be used to bring two sentences together:
Ma grand-mère s'appelle Marta. Elle est née en Espagne.
My grandmother is called Marta. She was born in Spain.

Ma grand-mère, qui s'appelle Marta, est née en Espagne.
My grandmother, who is called Marta, was born in Spain.

1 Which expression would you use in these circumstances?

> Tu rigoles!   Tu as raison!   Arrête!

a Someone is tickling you and you hate it. _____

b Someone asks you to lend them £500. _____

c Someone tells you how attractive you are. _____

d Someone is riding their bike towards a wall. _____

e Someone says two plus two equals four. _____

f Someone tells you something you really don't believe. _____

2 Write the words for the types of film into the boxes. What is the mystery word?

1   2   3   4   5   6

1 ☐☐☐☐☐☐☐ – ☐☐☐☐☐☐☐
2 ☐☐☐☐☐☐☐☐☐
3 ☐☐☐☐☐☐☐☐☐☐☐
4 ☐☐☐☐☐☐ ☐☐☐☐☐☐☐
5 ☐☐☐☐☐☐☐☐
6 ☐☐☐☐☐☐

The mystery word = _____

3 Look at the titles. What kinds of film do you think they are? Answer in French.

a Louis XIV _____

b Les Tigres de l'Inde _____

c Tra-la-la _____

d Les Gardiens de la Galaxie _____

e Lucas le Lapin _____

f Les Flics de Los Angeles _____

flic = cop (slang)

4 Read these expressions. Do they show agreement (A) or disagreement (D)?

a Arrête! A / D

b Mais non! A / D

c D'accord! A / D

d Tu as raison! A / D

e Tu rigoles! A / D

f Bonne idée! A / D

g C'est intéressant A / D

h C'est agaçant. A / D

5 In pairs. A suggests something to do starting with *Tu veux...* B agrees or disagrees using one of the phrases from the box below. Then swap roles.

d'accord   bonne idée   c'est intéressant   tu rigoles   ah non, pas ça   je ne suis pas d'accord

6 Read the conversation and answer the questions that follow.

Qu'est-ce qu'on commande? *Les Gardiens de la Galaxie*, peut-être?

Ah non, tu rigoles. La science-fiction, c'est trop bizarre pour moi. On peut plutôt commander *Lucas le Lapin*.

Arrête, Maeva! Tu n'aimes pas vraiment les animations?

Tu as raison. C'est pour les petits enfants, ça. *Tra-la-la*, peut-être?

Ah non, pas ça. Je déteste les comédies musicales. C'est trop ennuyeux.

Bof, alors, que penses-tu des *Flics de Los Angeles*?

Bonne idée, j'aime bien les films d'action. On le commande?

D'accord.

a Why does Maeva reject Abdou's first suggestion?

_____

b What is Maeva's first idea?

_____

c What kind of film is that?

_____

d Why does she change her mind?

_____

e What does Abdou think of *Tra-la-la*?

_____

f What kind of DVD do they eventually agree on?

_____

7 Join these pairs of sentences together using *qui*, as in the example. ⭐

a Le garçon s'appelle Jack. Il est né en 1874.
   Le garçon, qui s'appelle Jack, est né en 1874.

b Mon père a 39 ans. Il s'appelle Vincent.

_____

c Mon oncle habite à Paris. Il est malade.

_____

d Le film est très bizarre. Il s'appelle *Frisson*.

_____

e Le DVD est très long. Il est agaçant.

_____

f *Politique* est un documentaire. Il est intéressant.

_____

8 Translate your answers to exercise 7 into English. ⭐

_____

_____

_____

_____

• Pupil Book pages 114–115

Aujourd'hui, c'est le _____ . Il est _____ .

Langue et grammaire

Direct and indirect object pronouns

Remember that these pronouns go before the verb and that:

- The direct object pronoun for a masculine noun is *le* and for a feminine noun is *la*.
- The direct object pronoun for a plural noun is *les*.
- The indirect object pronoun for one person, whether they are male or female is *lui*.

I post the link on my blog.	*Je poste le lien sur mon blog.*
I post it on my blog.	*Je le poste sur mon blog.*
I take the photo.	*Je prends la photo.*
I take it.	*Je la prends.*

I take photos with my mobile phone.	*Je prends des photos avec mon portable.*
I take them with my mobile phone.	*Je les prends avec mon portable.*
I send my photos to my cousin.	*J'envoie mes photos à mon cousin/ma cousine.*
I send my photos to him/her.	*Je lui envoie mes photos.*

Perfect tense

When you are using the perfect tense, remember to check whether the past participle for the verb you want to use is irregular.

---

 1 The French translations for the expressions in the box are all in this grid. Find them.

to comment	link	photo	camera	to send
to post	slideshow	mobile phone	album	blog

a	c	o	m	m	e	n	t	e	r
p	t	i	n	o	p	a	a	l	b
p	j	s	l	i	o	b	l	o	g
a	l	b	u	m	r	b	i	y	p
r	r	p	h	o	t	o	e	b	o
e	e	m	a	d	a	c	n	l	s
i	g	q	e	l	b	s	c	v	t
l	s	m	w	i	l	r	h	m	e
e	n	v	o	y	e	r	r	s	r
f	s	l	i	d	e	s	h	o	w

2 Many French words to do with technology are 'cognates' (exactly the same as in English). Find the four cognates in exercise 1.

_____   _____   _____   _____

3 Shorten these sentences by using direct or indirect object pronouns (*le, la, les, lui*) to replace the underlined words, as in the example.

a Je prends <u>des photos</u>.   *Je les prends.* _____

a Manon partage <u>des photos</u>.   *Elle* _____

b Lucas partage <u>un album</u>.   *Il* _____

c Je regarde <u>la photo</u>.   _____

d Je poste <u>le lien</u>.   _____

e J'envoie les photos <u>à mon copain</u>.   _____

f Je montre une photo <u>à ma sœur</u>.   _____

4 Take turns with a partner to interview each other. Ask these questions:
- Tu aimes mon appareil photo?
- Tu prends des photos avec ton portable?
- Tu postes tes photos sur un blog?

> Try to use some direct object pronouns in your answers.

5 Fill in the gaps in this text, using words from the box below.

Je _____ (*take*) des photos avec mon _____ (*mobile*) et pour les _____ (*share*),

je les _____ (*post*) sur Facebook ou je les _____ (*save*) sur mon laptop. Souvent

je _____ (*upload*) les photos sur mon blog ou je les _____ (*send*) par email à ma famille.

Parfois je _____ (*create*) des slideshows pour mes copains.

| crée | envoie | partager | portable | poste | prends | sauvegarde | télécharge |

6 Translate this paragraph into English.

> L'année dernière, je suis allée en Italie avec mes parents. Nous avons visité beaucoup de monuments historiques, donc j'ai pris beaucoup de photos. J'ai posté quelques photos sur mon blog de vacances pour mes copains qui sont restés en France.

_____

_____

_____

7 Describe these photos using the perfect tense in the *nous* form. ⭐

a

b

c

a   aller   Paris   prendre des photos   tour Eiffel

_____

b   aller   plage   jouer   volley

_____

c   visiter   musée   regarder   œuvres

_____

8 Translate into French. ⭐

a I took some photos.   _____

b My brother is in Lille.   _____

c I sent the photos to him.   _____

d I share my photos with my friends. _____

e They like them.   _____